CW00386137

Needlepoint decor bags

Canvas, Colour, Stitch and Thread!

the excuse to do some more needlepoint

by Diana Parkes

GPL GEORGESON PUBLISHING LIMITED

Published by Georgeson Publishing Limited
P.O. Box 100-667, North Shore Mail Centre, New Zealand 1330.
Ph: 649 410 2079, Fax: 649 410 2069
Email: gpl@georgeson.co.nz, Web Site: www.georgeson.co.nz

This book is copyright. Except for the purpose of fair reviewing, no part of this publication may be reproduced or transmitted in any form or by any means, electronic or mechanical, including photocopying, recording, or any information storage and retrieval system, without permission in writing from the publisher. Infringers of copyright render themselves liable to prosecution.

We have made every effort to ensure that these instructions are accurate and complete. We cannot, however, be responsible for human error, typographical mistakes, or variations in individual work.

ISBN No. 0-9582105-9-4

© 2002 Diana Parkes

Editor:	Prue Georgeson
Photography:	Maria Sainsbury
Illustrations:	Diana Parkes
Layout:	Andreena Buckton, Noodle Design Corp.
Printed:	New Zealand

All projects in this book are designed by the author and are copyright reserved. They may not be reproduced in any printed form or taught in workshop environments.

The materials used in the designs in this book are available throughout the world from a wide range of stockists.

Should your local needlework store not have all of these items do not hesitate to contact us and we will advise you of alternative suppliers.

Acknowledgements

David and my family Lloyd, Rowan and Angela, and Lane
for their constant support

My students, past and present

Betty Logan who showed me the way

Creative Canvas Work

Take canvas
or congress cloth -
a thousand and a thousand
and a thousand
bits of nothingness
defined only by a thread

Lay out yarn,
floss, silk,
colour-coded, random,
blended with subtlety
or in shrieking contrast

Give substance to a dream
stitch by patterned stitch,
in image or icon,
symbol upon symbol
evoking metaphor.

Now,
before your eyes,
under your hand,
here
is something real.

Stella Mary Macdonald
Australia

Contents

All embroideries are by the author unless otherwise stated

Introduction

My main passion in life is embroidery. This association and commitment has remained undiminished for almost 30 years and life without those needles, threads and fabrics, is unthinkable and untenable. It impacts on my life in many ways and one aspect which has given me considerable pleasure is teaching embroidery. Through this involvement I have strengthened my knowledge and skills in embroidery and developed a consciousness that there is always more to learn, more to discover, and more roads to travel down. Each year my students and I set out on this journey together. As many of my students continue to return to these classes, I can only presume they recognize this journey too, along with all its pleasures and frustrations.

At the end of each year it is my challenge to arrange a programme for the following year. This is never an easy task as students will have already worked with many of the techniques in previous classes so new ideas are always being sourced. In 1997 I proposed DECOR BAGS as a topic with the bags made from any materials and using any technique. As a result we had a wide variety of small bags, ably embroidered and in most cases regarded as decorative rather than useful and practical. Further DECOR BAG classes followed with the focus on needlepoint and this is where it has remained.

These small attractive DECOR BAGS are wonderful vehicles for learning the needlepoint techniques, working through simple design formats and experimenting with numerous other embroidery combinations. They are small and as such are achievable in a limited time frame; they are colourful and fun and, as intended, are not practical as conventional bags. They are however ideal objects to hang on door handles, hat stands, or to display in and decorate rooms, hence the name DECOR BAGS. Good luck with your own journey, may it be a happy and satisfying one, peppered with just a few frustrations as this is when the boundaries are challenged, resulting in interesting and unique outcomes.

Diana Parkes, 2002

Important information (well worth reading....)

What is Needlepoint?   What is Canvas Work?

Confusion sometimes arises when using the terms Needlepoint and Canvas Work with some countries tending to favour one name to the other. The title given when you first came across this embroidery technique will probably remain your preferred description. Sometimes Needlepoint refers to works in Tent Stitch only, but the tendency nowadays seems to be to use it interchangeably with Canvas Work, thereby incorporating the large variety of stitch patterns and textures normally associated with this stitch technique.

I am sure I am not the only one who enjoys many forms of embroidery and the textile arts. Planning and starting yet another piece of Needlepoint (or Canvas Work) is like returning to that familiar comfortable fireside chair - it feels good and right and watching the many varied and complicated patterns and colours evolve as the work progresses, is immensely satisfying. Enjoy the feeling....

Canvas Colour

Traditionally single thread cotton canvases are supplied in white (interlocked) threads and brown (antique) threads, with thread counts varying from 10 to 18 threads per inch (tpi). Recently manufacturers have introduced a range of coloured canvases in black, yellow, cream, pink, light blue, navy, green, pewter and Christmas red and green with thread counts of 12, 14 and 18 tpi. For those who wish to use these, each design in the book has been given a coloured canvas option from the range available. This may result in a slightly different appearance to the illustrated DÉCOR BAGS.

When using a white canvas it is advisable to colour the canvas before stitching because the canvas is not always totally covered with the stitching. However, the colouring of the canvas with a background wash is optional, each bag may be worked on an unpainted canvas although some of the darker colours do work better on a painted or coloured canvas. The benefit of eliminating the whiteness of the canvas is illustrated on the next page.

Stitched sample of a crown   *Contrasts between uncoloured white canvas and a painted (coloured) canvas (household enamel spray paint). Stitches: Satin Stitch, Upright Cross, Tent Stitch and Alternating Cross Stitch, plus some machine stitching, applied painted felt and beads.*

If a brown canvas is selected additional colouring may not be necessary as the brown itself will help absorb colour contrasts.

There are four methods of colouring the canvas described in this book, they are:

(a)   fabric paint
(b)   transfer paint
(c)   transfer crayons
(b)   household enamel spray paint

The different qualities of each colouring agent are outlined along with the procedures for their use and the associated advantages, and disadvantages of each product. Select the DECOR BAG of your choice from the designs offered then refer back to the correct page for the colouring agent specified and follow the instructions given. Some quick experiments on a scrap of canvas will ensure you obtain a good result. However you will find that most of this colour is eventually covered in the stitching process.

notes

Canvas

All the DECOR BAGS in this book are worked on 14 threads per inch (tpi) white interlocked canvas. Cut the canvas to the required size then tape the cut edges with masking tape to prevent fraying and to avoid embroidery threads catching on the raw cut edges while you are stitching. Selvedge edges *do not* need to be taped. Never use your best sewing scissors for cutting any canvas as it will eventually blunt the cutting edges.

To frame or not to frame

Needlepoint is traditionally worked with the canvas secured in a frame to avoid distortion during the stitching process. Despite many years of doing this myself and instructing others to do likewise, I must confess all these bags were simply held in the hand while stitching. Because they are relatively small the canvas did not need to be scrunched and the shapes did not distort. However, if you prefer to work your piece in a slate/stretcher frame or a simple home-made frame as illustrated below, the decision is yours .... Canvas should be taut when framed either way.

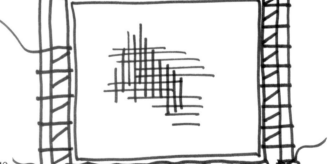

Slate or Stretcher frame
1. Cover edges of canvas with masking tape
2. Stitch top and bottom edges to frame tape
3. Firmly lace to sides

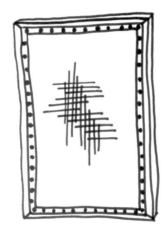

Home made frame
1. Nail wood together to required size.
2. Cover edges of canvas with masking tape
3. Staple or use thumb tacks to secure canvas to frame.

Needles

A Tapestry Needle #22 seems to accommodate all the thread types used. A tapestry needle has a large eye and a blunt point so that the canvas and other threads are not split while stitching. A finer crewel needle is needed when sewing in the linings and a beading needle is required for the beading.

Threads

DMC Perle 5 was the thread most commonly used for stitching all the DECOR BAGS. It is a mercerized cotton thread which is freely available in a very large colour range. It comes in a twisted hank with a paper loop at each end. I always remove these, cut one thread at the knot and wind the thread on to a plastic thread disk with the numbered paper loop tucked under the threads for easy reference. Some people like to remove the papers, open out the hank and cut through every thread at one point; these can then be twisted or plaited - each thread is lifted from the looped end with a needle and removed from the bunch.

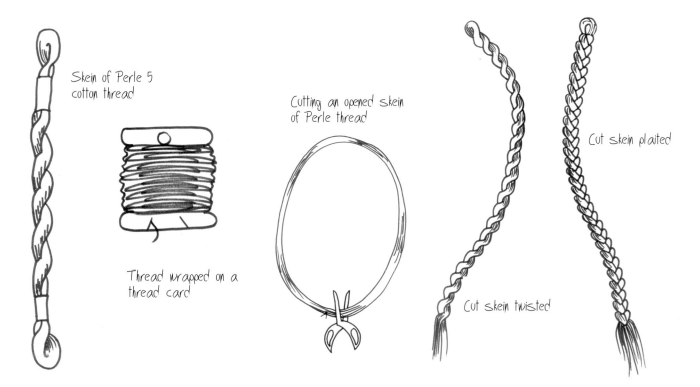

Skein of Perle 5 cotton thread

Thread wrapped on a thread card

Cutting an opened skein of Perle thread

Cut skein twisted

Cut skein plaited

There are many other threads that may also be used to achieve interesting textures and effects. I particularly like the Kreinik Tapestry Braid #12 which has a similar thickness to the DMC Perle 5 and offers that little bit of sparkle and accent. I also use Coton a broder 16 (three threads of stranded cotton may be used in its place).

Ribbons may be stitched into the patterns and of course beads added as well. I always keep my threads in colour boxes with any and every type of thread included in the colour range ie all reds together, all blues etc, no matter what their make and type. I find I am looking first for a colour, then a specific type within that colour range. Because I am always choosing my own colours this works very well but for those concentrating on specific charts with stated colours, it is probably best to keep them in numerical order or to follow the manufacturer's chart.

notes

Items used in making a DECOR BAG

Canvas
Masking Tape
DEKA Silks / brushes / sponge
Transfer Crayons / paper
Household spray paint
Polysol Dyes
Iron

Tacking thread
Needles
Silk Lining Fabric
Scissors
Embroidery threads - Perle 5, Kreinik
Beads
Ribbons

Samples stitched on backgrounds coloured using the four different methods

Canvas coloured with a wash of DEKA Silk fabric paints.
Stitches: Double Cross, threads and beads held down with
Satin Stitch

Canvas coloured with Polysol Transfer Paints.
Stitches: Woven Cross Stitch Laced, Tent Stitch, Woven Satin
Stitch, Mosaic Stitch Variation with Upright Cross

Canvas coloured with Crayola Transfer Crayons.
Stitches: Alternating Cross Stitch, Blackberry Stitch, Diamond
Eyelet Variation, straight stitch borders, beads

Canvas sprayed with household spray enamel.
Stitches: Tent Stitch, Satin Stitch, Double Upright Cross,
Woven Cross Stitch Laced, Rhodes Stitch Variation

Initial central tacking

Central tacked line on canvas over and under four threads

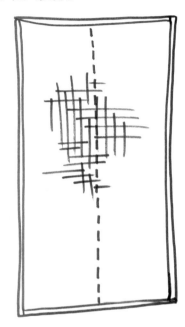

Tacking for front   Tacking for back

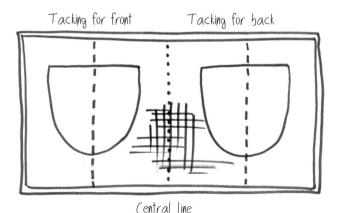

Central line

Stitching

Use a thread length no longer than 50 cm (20") to avoid stressing the thread as it moves in and out of the canvas. The metallic threads are best cut somewhat shorter e.g. 40 cm (15") as their threads are more delicate. See page 62 for starting and finishing threads.

Tacking

Some old habits are good and a quickly tacked central line in your canvas piece ensures the correct placement of the chart. Fold the canvas in half to determine the centre, start tacking in this fold and stitch over and under four threads of the canvas. This tacking may be removed as soon as you feel confident the design for your DÉCOR BAG is centred. Some of the bags (Summer House Decor Bag, Music Room Decor Bag and Drawing Room Decor Bag) have a separate front and back and a central tacked line is worked for both pieces.

Lining Fabric

You may choose to colour the lining fabric for your bag at the same time as the canvas. This results in a co-ordinated finish and certainly saves searching for just that right colour for the lining. I always use a silk pongee fabric as it looks attractive and feels nice but many other fabrics are suitable. If you do not wish to colour your own lining, searching through your own fabric scraps or shopping for just the right match is an enjoyable part of the process.

Cords and Tassels

The cords and tassels are all interchangeable. See page 76 onwards for a selection of simple cords and tassels.

Beads and Ribbons

Where beads have been used, specific types/brands/colours have been mentioned. If these are not readily available your own selection will be completely satisfactory.
Ribbons are freely available. The width required is specified but use whatever is available in your personal stash or at your local needlework store.

NEEDLEPOINT STITCHES

The stitch charts on pages 61-73 give stitches that have been enjoyed by generations of needle-workers and you may already be familiar with some of them. However by rearranging different aspects of the stitches they are often given a totally new appearance, especially when they are built into complex overall patterns and textures. Stitch names vary between countries and I have given some new titles simply to assist in their identification. They are co-ordinated into groups and types and in many cases given several interpretations. When you are creating your own DECOR BAG you will find this presentation a tremendous help in your stitch selections.

IRONING / PRESSING YOUR STITCHED CANVAS

You may wish to press your stitched canvas before constructing it into a DECOR BAG. Place the stitched canvas face down on to a padded ironing board, cover the canvas with a clean cloth and press gently with a steam iron. Allow canvas to dry completely before commencing construction.

GALLERY SECTION

Page 78 shows additional DECOR BAGS made by myself and others. These show some of the creative possibilities that may be obtained when stitching these delightful bags using the techniques shown in this book. Their small format makes them readily achievable with plenty of opportunities to make a pleasing statement.

DESIGNING YOUR OWN DECOR BAG

On completion of your selected DECOR BAG/s I hope you will be inspired to design your own DECOR BAG. Pages 84-87 give guidance and ideas for this.

COLOUR

I have stitched my DÉCOR BAGS in a variety of colour schemes. You may wish to choose your own colours and pages 82-83 give some thoughts and ideas on developing your own colour schemes. Because these are DECOR BAGS I suggest when making your own colour selection that you start with the decoration and items in an existing room and choose colours to coordinate, then you will have a home for your bag. Have confidence when selecting your own colours, from my experience most people handle colour much better than they would acknowledge.

OTHER WORKS ON CANVAS

Items on page 79 are not DECOR BAGS but are other works on canvas. Their intentions and inspirations are included for your contemplation.

notes

Colouring Canvas

(fabric paints, transfer paints, transfer crayons, household spray enamel)

It is not always necessary to colour the canvas before stitching (and a wide range of coloured canvas is now available). Colouring your own canvas does add a *colour depth* as well as a *colour contrast* to your work with the advantage of creating subtle colours not available in commercially dyed canvas. The old saying that no canvas should be showing in your finished work, *definitely does not apply here.* Many of the stitches do not totally cover the background canvas and some canvas is deliberately left exposed. The lining fabric will appear through areas of unstitched canvas on the finished DÉCOR Bag adding another colour dimension to your piece. Colouring the canvas with any of the techniques described here is no more than a simple colour wash. Anything more complicated is eliminated when the canvas is eventually stitched. These colouring procedures do not alter the properties of the canvas.

Initial Preparation Procedures:

1. Place masking tape around the raw edges of your canvas once it is cut to the size required.

2. Cover the table with newspaper or plastic to protect the working surface.

3. When using the DEKA Silks you may consider placing your lining fabric underneath so that excess paint will soak the fabric as well which will result in a perfectly matching lining. With the Transfer Paints and Transfer Crayons the colours will drift through the canvas holes when ironing and appear as a spotted grid. The fabric may be re-coloured further with the Transfer Paints and Transfer Crayons. Do not spray lining fabric with household spray enamel as it will result in a stiff fabric not really suitable for a lining. You do not have to colour your own lining fabric, if you prefer you may use any matching commercially dyed fabric.

4. When using Transfer Paints or Transfer Crayons the colour is transferred with a hand held iron. If you own an ironing press or have access to one, use it as it will distribute a high, even heat at considerable pressure and the colours on the canvas will be stronger than with a hand held iron. However keep checking the paper and canvas to avoid scorching.

5. Refer to *Procedure* for each bag for further instructions in colouring the canvas for each specific DECOR BAG.

DEKA Silk Paints

Similar textile paints are available under various brand names.

These textile paints are extremely versatile. They are made for all textiles, are water based and have a very good range of colours which are inter-mixable. They may be applied to natural and synthetic fabrics and only require heat setting with an iron to be colour fast.

Procedure

Refer Initial Preparation Procedures page 14.

Hold the canvas under a running cold water tap or soak it in a tub before painting so the paints will blend better. A natural coloured lining fabric may be placed under the canvas before painting as this will absorb surplus paint which passes through the holes in the canvas. DEKA Silks may be applied to the canvas with a paintbrush, sponge brush or a piece of sponge. When the colouring is to your liking, leave the canvas to dry, before heat setting the colour on the canvas (and lining fabric) with a hot dry iron for at least two minutes.

Advantages:

1. A very good inter-mixable colour range which allows for colour mixing prior to painting as well as for colour blending directly on the canvas.
2. Water based so colours may be made less intense by adding water.
3. With the lining fabric placed underneath to soak up excess dye, you will have a matching lining fabric.
4. DEKA Silks may be used for other projects as well as they are so versatile e.g. silk painting, backgrounds for other embroidery projects etc.
5. Non-tonic, and have an unlimited shelf life.

Disadvantages:

1. The painted canvas needs to be left to dry before heat setting.

notes

notes

Transfer Paints

These paints come in powder form (Polysol Transfer Dyes) and in a ready-made liquid form (DEKA Iron On Paints). They are designed to work on synthetic or synthetic-blend fabrics where the colours obtain maximum brightness; however, they do also work on white canvas which is cotton, albeit somewhat less intensely.

Procedure

Refer Initial Preparation Procedures page 14.

To use Polysol Transfer Dyes which come in powder form, place a small amount of powder into a flat dish/container then add small amounts of hot water to dissolve the powder. This is a trial and error approach - less water, more powder will result in a stronger colour; more water, less powder will give a paler colour. DEKA Iron On ready-mixed paints are of course ready to use immediately. Paint colours onto paper. Leave to dry thoroughly. Place a firm surface ie cardboard or a telephone book on to an ironing board or table, cover with a piece of scrap paper to avoid staining the underneath surface then place lining fabric on this. Place canvas on top of the lining fabric, then position painted paper face down on to the canvas. Using a very hot dry iron, press the back of the paper firmly and thoroughly while keeping the iron moving. The paints will transfer on to the canvas, repeat for deeper colours. If you have an ironing press use it but keep checking to avoid scorching the paper and canvas. The canvas is now ready for stitching. The lining fabric may require further colouring either by further Transfer Dyes or fabric paints.

Advantages:

1. Easy to use and the canvas is ready to use immediately.
2. Polysol Transfer Dyes powders will last for sometime when mixed with water although eventually they will become paler so it is advisable to mix only small amounts each time.
3. Ideal for use with children.
4. Non-tonic, water-based and fade resistant.

Disadvantages:

1. Difficult to obtain.
2. There is a delay while the painted paper dries thoroughly, although this can be helped by placing in the sun or using a hair drier.
3. Colours are limited but they mix together very well to create new colours.
4. The colours painted on to the paper may appear uninteresting but experience will show that once the heat is applied they will appear much brighter.
5. Colours will appear more transparent than other colour applications ie fabric paints.
6. Best used on synthetic fabric where colours will be stronger than on natural fibre fabrics.

Transfer Crayons

A selection of eight colours produced by *Crayola Crayons.* These may be difficult to obtain but are available. Transfer Crayons are made specifically to be used on synthetic (or synthetic-blend fabrics) and embroidery canvas is usually cotton.

Procedure

Refer Initial Preparation Procedures page 14 .
Apply crayons with considerable pressure to good quality white paper ie photocopying paper, slightly larger than the pieces required for your DECOR BAG. Place a firm surface ie cardboard or a telephone book on to an ironing board or table, then cover with a piece of scrap paper or your lining fabric to avoid staining the surface underneath. Place canvas on to the scrap paper, then the crayon application paper face down on the canvas. Using a very hot dry iron, press the back of the paper firmly and thoroughly. Keep the iron moving to avoid steam hole markings. If you have an ironing press use it but keep checking to avoid scorching the paper and canvas. The crayons will transfer on to the canvas, repeat for deeper colours. The canvas is now ready for stitching.

Advantages:

1. Easy and non-messy to use.
2. The canvas is ready to use immediately.
3. Ideal for use with children.
4. Non-tonic.

Disadvantages:

1. Difficult to obtain.
2. Colours are limited to eight but they can be mixed by applying one colour over another.
3. Colours may appear somewhat paler than expected (see above) but with the addition of stitching and the eventual lining being placed behind the canvas, the outcome will be satisfactory.
4. Best used on synthetic fabrics where the colours will be stronger than on natural fibre fabrics.

For those who like experimenting, the transfer crayons may be worked directly on to the canvas (the red and blue sampler on page 65 is coloured this way). Place canvas on a protective surface and colour with crayons. Place a piece of fabric on top of the canvas and iron with a hot iron. The crayons on the canvas will fix, while the fabric will be a bonus as it takes on the image and colours used on the canvas. This fabric may be used as a co-ordinated lining or for another project altogether.

Household Spray Enamel

Many hardware DIY stores now stock small cans of spray paint at an affordable price. The colour range is limited but also includes favourites such as gold, silver and copper. Their application is simple and they offer a good coverage of the canvas.

Procedure

Refer Initial Preparation Procedures page 14.

Spray paints are best applied when the canvas is held vertical. Cover the work area well with newspaper and support your canvas in a vertical position. Allow for good ventilation with open windows and doors to avoid fumes (a face mask will be necessary if you are intending to spray a large area). The room temperature should be approximately 21°C. Shake can of spray paint vigorously and again during spraying if doing a large area. Spray canvas in short bursts, at a distance of about 25cm (10") until the canvas is coloured to your satisfaction. Do not colour your fabric lining with this paint as the end result is not really suitable. (For further precautions read the instructions on the can). Leave to dry.

Advantages:

1. Easy to obtain, and affordable.
2. A good selection of colours which may be blended by overlaying colours when spraying on to the canvas.
3. Results achieved quickly.
4. No need to heat set, canvas is ready to stitch when paint is dry.

Disadvantages:

1. Fumes are strong so ventilation or a face mask is recommended.
2. Colours unable to be mixed prior to stitching.
3. Finished item may not be washable but as this is not a priority with DECOR BAGS this is not really a problem.
4. Spray cans contain hydrocarbons.

MORNING ROOM DECOR BAG (1)

Stillness, beginnings and expectations...

For additional detail refer to colour photograph page 21
Finished size 10 x 14.5 cm (4 x 6 in)

Materials

One piece of White Interlock Canvas 14 threads per inch (tpi) 20 cm x 35 cm (8"x 14")
Lining Fabric, cotton or silk, white or cream, 20 cm x 35 cm (8" x 14")
DEKA Silk Textile Paints: Colours   35.25 Rosenholz
                                  35.79 Rostbraun (or your own choices)
Alternative Canvas: Zweigart Hobby Art Canvas, Colour 409 Pink

Embroidery Threads and Other Things:

1 skein each   DMC Cotton Perle 5: Ecru, 340, 352, 725, 734,754.
                     DMC Stranded Cotton: 437 (use 3 threads), 959 (use 3 threads),
                     340 (1 thread only for sewing on beads)
                     DMC Metallic Embroidery Floss 5279 (use one strand),
1 pkt DMC General Beads V1-05-3746 Lavender
1 metre (1 yd) satin ribbon 6mm (1/4 in) wide to match DMC Cotton Perle 5: 352

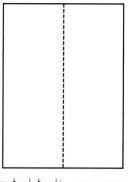

central tacking on canvas

To Colour your Canvas *see page 15*

Stitching *see pages 61-73*

To Begin

1.   Tack centre line lengthwise over and under four threads (ths).
2.   Start 4 cm (1 1/2") down from the top edge of the canvas with the top row of Tent Stitch using Stranded Cotton, 959 (3 ths and 1 strand of Metallic Embroidery Floss 5279). Work 30 stitches to the right then 30 to the left. This row establishes the side edges of the bag.
3.   Follow chart for colour placement. Stitches and threads to use are given in the text.

The chart gives only one side of the bag and will need to be continued below the centre side arrows in reverse order to complete the bag.

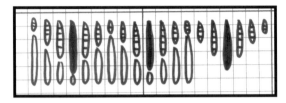

Row 3 & 5 Satin Stitch - Zigzag #1

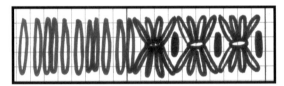

Row 7 Sheaf Stitch Variation #1

Row 1	**Tent Stitch - p71 (refer: To Begin 2, p20)**	Stranded cotton: 437 (3 ths only) + 1 strand 5279
Row 2	**Satin Stitch - p63**	Metallic Embroidery Floss: 5279, over 2 threads using 4 strands
Row 3	**Satin Stitch - Zigzag #1**	Perle 5: 754, Ecru, 725
Row 4	**Repeat Row 2**	
Row 5	**Satin Stitch - Zigzag #1**	Perle 5: 754, 734, 352
Row 6	**Repeat Row 2**	
Row 7	**Sheaf Stitch Variation #1**	Perle 5: 340,over 4 ths Straight St over 2 ths in between Sheaves using Stranded 959 (3 ths only)
Row 8	**Vertical bands occupying a depth of 24 ths, each band 12 ths wide, repeated five times**	

From the left:

Row 1	**Tent Stitch**	Perle 5: Ecru
Row 2	**Cross Stitch - p66**	Perle 5: 754, over 2 ths
Row 3	**Tent Stitch**	Stranded 959 (3 ths only)
Row 4	**Double Cross - p66**	Diagonal Cross Perle 5: 734, over 4 ths Upright Cross Perle 5: 725 One lavender bead sewn between the stitches.
Row 5	**Tent Stitch**	Stranded 959 (3 ths only)
Row 6	**Cross Stitch**	Perle 5: 352, over 2 ths
Row 7	**Tent Stitch**	Stranded 25: 427 (3 ths only) + 1 strand 5279
Row 9	**Satin Stitch couching over ribbon**	Ribbon & Perle 5: 340, 2 stitches together over 4 ths, 3 ths apart couching apricot ribbon in place

Row 9 Satin Stitch couching over ribbon

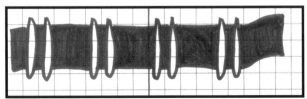

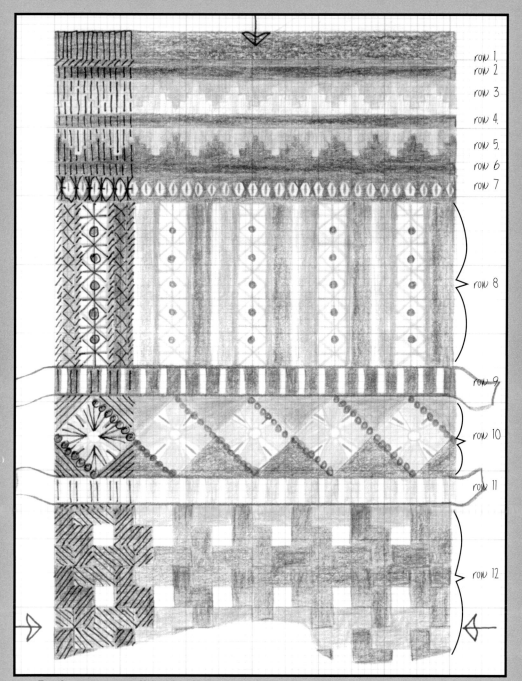

row 1.
row 2
row 3
row 4.
row 5.
row 6
row 7

row 8

row 9

row 10

row 11

row 12

key

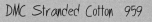

DMC Perle 5: 340
DMC Stranded Cotton 959
DMC Stranded Cotton 437
DMC Metallic Embroidery Floss 5279
DMC Perle 5: 725

DMC Perle 5: 734
DMC Perle 5: 352
DMC Perle 5: Ecru
DMC Perle 5: 754

- **Each square on this chart represents one thread of fabric**
- The ribbon is shown by uncoloured squares on the chart and the ribbon ends are shown extended at the sides, they will be stitched into the side seams.

Morning Room Décor Bag 1

21

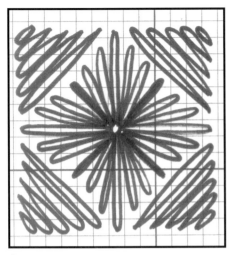

Row 10 Cushion Corners

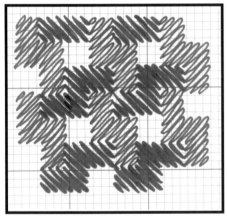

Row 12 Interlocking Blocks

This section comprises 5 squares each 12 x 12 ths, repeat the following:

Row 10	**Cushion Corners**	Perle 5: 754 (top half) & 352 (bottom) and *Diamond Eyelet* Perle 5: 734, contrast stitches (in the middle of each side) Stranded cotton: 959, 3 ths.
	Rows of beads	Attach 7 lavender beads, on opposite sides of each diamond. See page 76 for stitching rows of beads
Row 11	**Repeat Row 9**	Ribbon & Perle 5: 725
Row 12	**Interlocking Blocks**	Perle 5: 340, 754, 352 (this results in an unstitched square in the pattern).

Assembling the Bag

1. Trim the sides of bag leaving six threads of the canvas as seam allowance. Trim top edges leaving eight threads of the canvas.

2. With right sides together fold bag at base line and, matching stitch patterns, machine stitch side seams as close as possible to the stitch patterns.

3. Nick seam allowance at base, fold and slip stitch each seam allowance back to wrong side of embroidery.

4. Turn over four threads at the top edge of the bag and work *Buttonhole Stitch* in Perle 5: 798 over the two layers. Then work *Raised Stem Band* (same colour) on the front side of the *Buttonhole Stitch* until it is covered, approximately six rows, continue on the inside until it is also covered (see p75 for stitches).

5. Cord: Take a 1.5 metre (60") length of each of the Perle 5 threads, plus one of Metallic Thread and use these to make a twisted cord. Using the same threads make two tassels (finished length of 5cm/2in). The cord is threaded through the tassels and the ends are secured with binding before covering the side loops with *Buttonhole Stitch* and decorating with beads. The cord and tassels have been finished as described in (e) FINISHINGS, AND OTHER THINGS page 81. Attach to side seams.

6. Cut a piece of lining fabric 14 cm x 30cm (5 1/2" x 12"), sew side seams. Place inside bag, fold under top edge and blind stitch to the base of the *Buttonhole Stitch* on the inside.

MEDITERRANEAN ROOM DECOR BAG (2)
Azure sea, geraniums and cobbled streets...

For additional detail refer to the coloured photograph page 24
Finished size 12 x 15cm (5 x 6in)

Materials

One piece of White Interlock Canvas 14 threads per inch (tpi) 20 cm x 40 cm (8" x 16")
Lining Fabric, cotton or silk, white or cream, 20 cm x 40 cm (8" x 16")
DEKA Silk Textile Paints: Colours   35.58 Turkisblau
                                       35.49 Blau
                                       35.39 Violett (or your own selection)
Alternative Canvas: Zweigart Hobby Art Canvas, Colour 503 light blue

Embroidery Threads and other things:

1 skein each   DMC Cotton Perle 5: 327, 676, 798, 3731, 3746, 3765
                     DMC Embroidery Rayon 30943
                     DMC Metallic Embroidery Floss 5283
Purple beads to co-ordinate

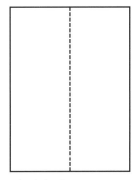

central tacking on canvas

To Colour your Canvas *see page 15*

Stitching *see pages 61-73*

To Begin

1.   Tack centre line lengthwise over and under four threads (ths).
2.   Measure down 4 cm (1 1/2") from the top of the canvas and start stitching with a row of Satin Stitch over two threads in DMC Perle 3746 and work 34 stitches to the right, then 34 stitches to the left. This row establishes the side edges of the bag.
3.   Follow chart for colour placement. Stitches and threads to use are given in the text.

The chart gives only one side of the bag and will need to be continued below the centre side arrows in reverse order to complete the bag.

key

	DMC Perle 5: 3731	DMC Perle 5: 676	
	DMC Perle 5: 327	DMC Perle 5: 3765	
	DMC Perle 5: 3746	DMC Embroidery Rayon 30943	
	DMC Perle 5: 798	DMC Metallic Embroidery Floss 5283	

Mediterranean Décor Bag 2

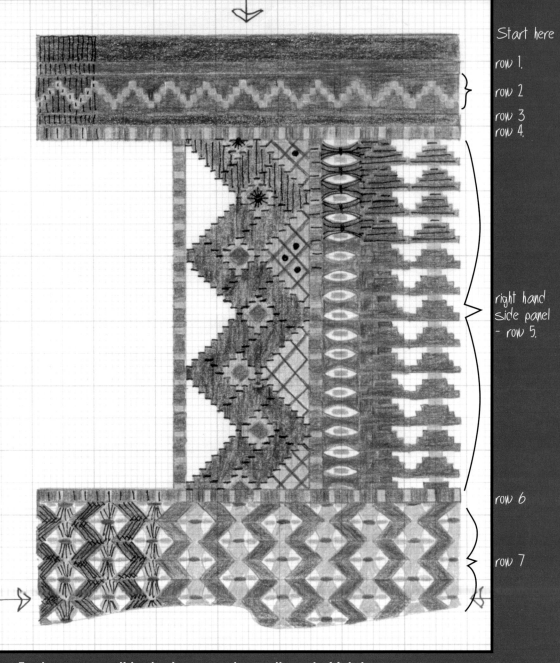

Start here

row 1.

row 2

row 3

row 4.

right hand side panel - row 5.

row 6

row 7

• Each square on this chart represents one thread of fabric

Row 1	**Satin Stitch - p63 (refer: To Begin 2 p23)**	Perle 5: 3746, over 2 ths
Row 2	**Satin Stitch Zigzag #2 - p63**	Top zigzag Perle 5: 327, centre zigzag Metallic Embroidery Floss 5283 using 4 strands, lower zigzag Perle 5: 3731
Row 3	**Satin Stitch**	Perle 5: 798, over 2 ths
Row 4	**Satin Stitch Couched over threads**	Two laid threads of Perle 5: 3765, Satin stitch over 2 ths every second canvas hole, alternating Perle 5: 3731 & 676
Row 5	Vertical bands occupying a depth of 53 threads.	

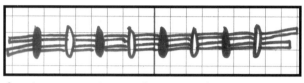

Row 4 Satin Stitch Couched over threads

Right hand side panel

Milanese Straight

The top and bottom stitches in this panel share the same holes of canvas used by the couched thread above and below. Working from right to left following the chart stitch using Perle 5: 3746, with the top stitch over 2 ths in Embroidery Rayon 30943.

Next row Perle 5: 327 with top stitch over 2 ths in Perle 5: 798. A part-Milanese Straight stitch is fitted along the inner edge using Perle 5: 3731 see chart p24.

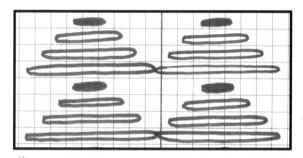

Milanese Straight

Sheaf Stitch #2

Perle 5: 3746 over 6 ths and a single straight stitch over 2 ths in the gaps using 6 strands of Metallic Embroidery Floss 5283

Satin Stitch Couching

Repeat Row 4 above but stitch it vertically

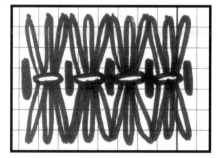

Sheaf Stitch #2

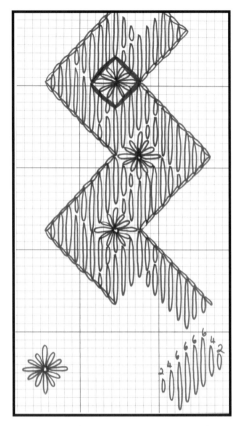

Central Band Satin Stitch Zigzag and Diamond Eyelets

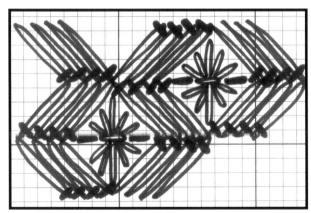

Row 7 Diagonal Tied Composite Stitch

Central band:

Satin Stitch Zigzag	Perle 5: 798. Stitches worked over a maximum of six threads
Diamond Eyelets	Perle 5: 3731 over 6 ths, then outlined with straight stitches in Perle 5: 676
Blackberry Stitch - p66	Upright cross over 4 ths using Embroidery Rayon 30943, then Cross Stitch over 2 ths in Perle 5: 327
Back Stitch - p75	Zigzag Satin Blocks are outlined with Back Stitch in Metallic Embroidery Floss 5283 using all 6 strands.

Add beads to each of the *Diamond Eyelets* and three within each of the *Blackberry Stitch* sections.

Left hand side panel - Complete as for right side reversing order of rows.

Row 6   **Repeat Row 4**

Row 7   **Diagonal Tied Composite Stitch**

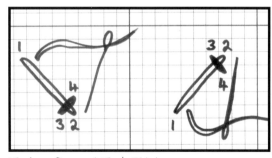

To begin Diagonal Tied Stitch

Work 10 complete rows in all, so that 5 will appear on each side of the bag. Start with *Diagonal Tied Stitch* worked first using Perle 5: 3731 then 798, stitch in alternating rows, creating diamonds in which a shaped *Sheaf Stitch* is worked using Embroidery Rayon 30943, tied down with one horizontal straight stitch using Perle 5: 327. A small horizontal stitch over 2 ths is placed either side, in Metallic Embroidery Floss 5283 using 6 strands.

Assembling the Bag

1. Trim the sides of the bag leaving a seam allowance of six threads of canvas. Trim top edges leaving eight threads of canvas.

2. Fold bag at base line, with right sides together and matching stitch patterns, machine stitch side seams.

3. Nick seam allowance at fold and slip stitch each seam allowance back to wrong side of embroidery.

4. Turn over four threads at the top edge of the bag and work *Buttonhole Stitch* in Perle 5: 798 over the two layers. Then work *Raised Stem Band* (same colour) on the front side of the Buttonhole Stitch until it is covered, approximately six rows, continue on the inside till covered (see p75 for stitches).

5. Cord: Using 9 x 1.2 metre (47 in) lengths of a selection of the threads left over from the stitching, plait (basic three plait) threads together and knot 3 cm (1 1/4") from each end. Slip stitch this cord to the side seams of the bag starting with the knots at the bottom corners. (See FINISHINGS, AND OTHER THINGS pages 74-81).

6. Cut a piece of lining fabric 14 x 30cm (5 1/2"x 12"), sew side seams.
   Place inside bag, fold under top edge and blind stitch to the base of the *Buttonhole Stitch* on the inside.

notes

notes

SUMMER HOUSE DECOR BAG (3)

Soft breezes, the scent of flowers and cool drinks...

Refer to colour photograph page 29 for additional detail.
Finished length including tassel 23 cm (9 in) Width, at widest point 13cm (5 1/4 in)

Materials

One piece of White Interlock Canvas 14 threads per inch (tpi) 25 cm x 35 cm (10"x 14")
Crayola Transfer Crayons: Yellow, Orange, Burnt Sienna
Lining Fabric: 0.5 m (1/2 yd) in a colour to co-ordinate with the thread colours. I painted a piece of pongee silk using the DEKA Silk paints. If using scrap fabric, sufficient is needed to cut two B's plus two bias strips, one 5 x 15 cm (2" x 6") and the other 5 x 55 cm (2" x 22").
Alternative Canvas: Zweigart Hobby Art Canvas, Colour 409, Pink

Embroidery Threads and other things:

1 skein each   DMC Perle 5: 316, 677, 922, 977, 3348
Kreinik Metallic Tapestry Braid #12: 007
1 pkt DMC General Beads V1-06-0971 to match thread colour DMC 922, orange

To Colour your Canvas *see page 17*

Stitching *see pages 61-73*

To Begin

1. Draw template shapes A B C from the chart (page 74) on to a sheet of A4 paper. Colour the shapes on the paper using the transfer crayons.
2. Transfer colours to canvas with iron then using an ordinary felt pen in a colour similar to the crayon work, trace template lines on to your canvas. Remember that your shapes will have been reversed on the canvas.
3. Tack centre line through the shapes.
4. Follow chart for colour placement. Stitches and threads to use are given in the text.

All stitch patterns on this bag should be worked up to the marked shape on the canvas of the bag which includes the seam allowance and not beyond as the canvas will be cut at this point during construction. The narrow gap between the split sections must not have any stitches across it as it will be cut here also.

Summer House Décor Bag 3

Diamond Eyelets/Half Rhodes Stitches

Section B - front

Work central vertical band (20 ths wide) from left to right.

(a) Sheaf Stitch #3 - p69   over 4 ths Perle 5: 316. Convert each 3 satin stitches into a Sheaf using Tapestry Braid #12: 007. Work 2 Satin Stitches over 2 ths in the gap created Perle 5: 977

(b) Alternating Satin Stitch - p63   Perle 5: 677 & 3348 work 2 stitches over 2 ths in each colour

(c) Diamond Eyelets   This band is 8 ths wide. Stitch *Diamond Eyelets* in Perle 5: 922, 6 ths wide at the points, leaving 1 th. spare each side and 3 ths below and above.

(d) Half Rhodes Stitches   Perle 5: 316 work Half Rhodes Stitches across the full 8 ths, between each Diamond Eyelet. Half Rhodes will consist of 10 overlapping stitches.
Tie centres down with a Straight Stitch Tapestry Braid #12: 007

Repeat (b) then (a) above.

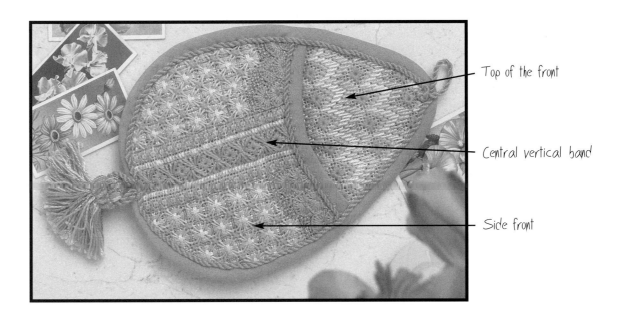

Top of the front

Central vertical band

Side front

Buttonhole Half Round Eyelets - p69

Perle 5: 316, 8 ths wide and 4 deep, to the top right and left of the central vertical band (see chart). Place a bead in the centre hole of each *Buttonhole Half Round Eyelet* Beads V1-06-0971 Orange

Upright Cross -p66

Place *Upright Cross* in spaces between *Buttonhole Half Round Eyelets* Tapestry Braid #12: 007

Woven Cross Stitch Combination

Work in side panels slightly below *Buttonhole Half Round Eyelets* (see chart)

(a) Cross Stitches (work first)

Perle 5: 922, over 2 ths with intervals of 5 ths in between

(b) Large Double Diagonal Crosses

Perle 5: 3348 see chart

(c) Double Upright Cross

Perle 5: 677, over 7 ths

(d) Interlaced Circles

Perle 5: 977, 2 journeys

(e) Side Straight Stitch

Tapestry Braid #12: 007, over 3 threads

Weaving Stitch - p69

Tapestry Braid #12: 007, work *Weaving Stitch* in gap between *Buttonhole Half Round Eyelets* and *Woven Cross Stitch*

notes

Woven Cross Stitch Combination

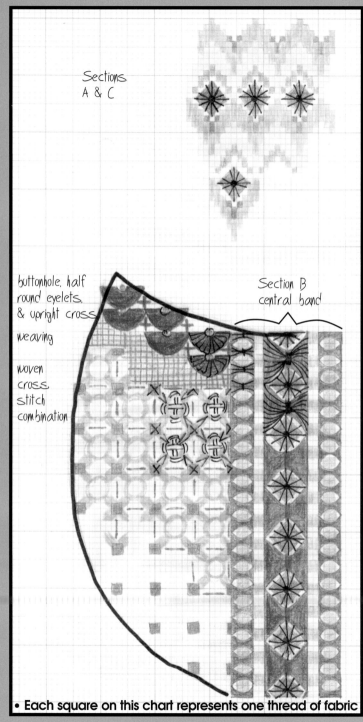

Sections
A & C

buttonhole, half
round eyelets,
& upright cross

weaving

woven
cross
stitch
combination

Section B
central band

• **Each square on this chart represents one thread of fabric**

Sections 'A' top of the front and 'C' back

Work the *Florentine/Eyelet Variation* stitch on the smallest split section 'A' (this becomes the top of the inside lining) and on the large whole shape 'C' (which is the back of the bag). Centre one of the *Eyelets* over the central tacking line and extend pattern from there.

Florentine/Eyelet Variation

Diamond Eyelet Perle 5: 922 6 threads (ths) across at points. (The space for the Diamond Eyelets is actually 8 ths across at the points but one thread of the canvas on all sides is unstitched.)

Broken line of Satin Stitch above Eyelet Perle 5: 977

Top line Florentine Stitch Perle 5: 677, over 4 ths

Broken line of Satin Stitch below Eyelet Tapestry Braid #12: 007

Lower line Florentine Stitch Perle 5: 3348, over 4 ths

key

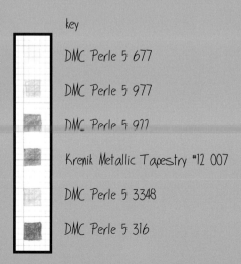

DMC Perle 5: 677

DMC Perle 5: 977

DMC Perle 5: 977

Krenik Metallic Tapestry #12 007

DMC Perle 5: 3348

DMC Perle 5: 316

Florentine/Eyelet Variation

Assembling the Bag

1. Machine stitch along the felt pen line around the outer edge of each shape. Trim away all excess canvas to the outside of this line/stitching.

2. Cut two shapes from the lining fabric using shape B. Make a series of small cuts into the concave seam allowance of one piece; pin and stitch to the convex edge of the top canvas piece 'A'. Turn and press. Place this on to the back canvas 'C', matching cut edges (reverse sides together). Machine stitch together close to the cut edge.

3. Place the second piece of lining, cut from shape B, behind the front panel and machine stitch together close to the cut edge. Cut a bias strip from the lining fabric 5 x 15 cm (2 x 6 in). Pin and stitch to the wrong side of the top edge of the front panel 'B', then fold over to the front side, turn under seam allowance, slipstitch to the front side.

4. Make a twisted cord from Perle 5: 922 15cm long (6") and stitch along the inside edge of the binding. Add a row of orange beads spaced evenly above the cord.

5. Sew front and back together carefully. Cut a bias strip from the lining fabric 5 x 55 cm (2 x 22 in); sew to the back edge of the bag, placing seam at centre bottom. Fold bias strip to the front, turn under seam allowance and slip stitch in place leaving a section near the base unstitched. Make a twisted cord from Perle 5: 922 70cm (27") long and stitch to the inside edge starting at the base, and manipulating the cord to make a loop at the top of the bag. Attach a tassel (finished length 5cm/2in and made using all the threads) at the base (the ends of the cord are placed within the bias strip). Complete the slip stitching of the bias binding.

See FINISHINGS, AND OTHER THINGS for how to make tassels and cords, pages 74-81.

notes

Music Room Décor Bag 4

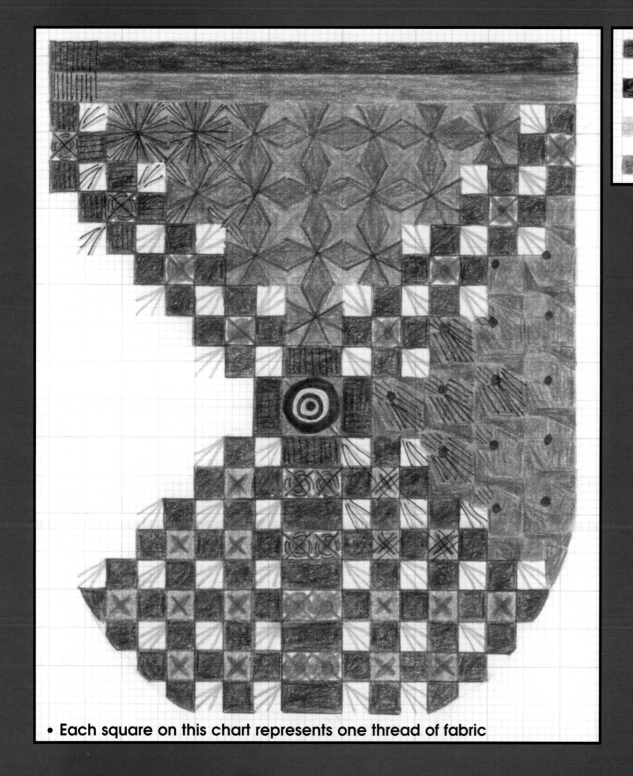

• **Each square on this chart represents one thread of fabric**

DMC Perle 5: 809   DMC Perle 5: 930

DMC Perle 5: 310   DMC Perle 5: 3041

DMC Perle 5: 830   Kreinik Metallic
                    Tapestry #12 007

DMC Perle 5: 935

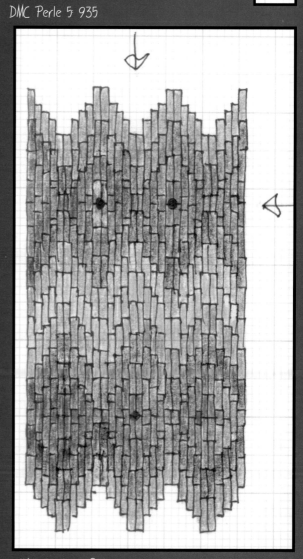

GUSSET CHART
Arrows indicate centre of chart

35

notes

MUSIC ROOM DECOR BAG (4)

Leather chairs, solitude and sweet melodies...

For additional detail refer to colour photograph page 34
Finished size   13 x16cm (6 x 5in)

Materials

One piece of White Interlock Canvas 14 tpi 30 cm x 45 cm (12" x 18")
Lining Fabric, cotton or silk, white or cream, 30 cm x 45 cm (12" x 18")
DEKA Silk Textile Paints: Colours   35.71 Grunoliv
                                                            35.90 Schwarz (or your own selection)
Alternative Canvas: Zweigart Hobby Art Canvas, Colour 095, Black

Embroidery Threads and other things:

1 skein each   DMC Cotton Perle 5: 809, 830, 930, 935, 3041
                        Kreinik Tapestry Braid #12: 007
2 skeins   DMC Cotton Perle 5: 310
Jet black beads 2-3mm
2 black buttons 10mm (1/2")
3 1/2 metres/yards black cord

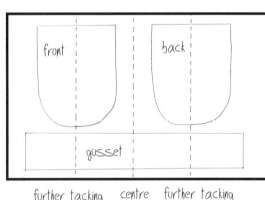

front   back

gusset

further tacking   centre   further tacking
centre of   tacking   centre of
each half   each half

To Colour your Canvas   *see page 15*

Stitching   *see pages 61-73*

To Begin

1. Mark the centre of the canvas and the centres of each half lengthwise, see layout chart.
2. Follow chart p35 for colour placement. Stitches and threads to use are given in the text.

The chart gives the front, repeat for the back. The gusset is stitched separately.

Front

Measure down 4 cm (1 1/2") from the top of the front and back pieces of canvas and starting at the top left hand side using Perle 5: 310, work all the *Alternating Satin Stitch Blocks* plus the large blocks in the centre lower half. This will give the basic structure for the front and back pieces of the bag.

Satin Stitch Blocks Alternating - p64 using Perle 5: 310 each five satin stitches over four threads (ths), mentioned above.

Ray Stitch - p64 work in Perle 5: 830 in between the Alternating Satin Stitch Blocks

Rhodes Stitch Variation in centre top triangle first using Perle 5: 809 overlaid with Perle 5: 310 then *Rhodes Cross Stitch* in the remaining spaces Perle 5: 3041.

Offset Mosaic is worked in two side triangles using Perle 5: 3041 for the smaller corner blocks, Perle 5: 930 for the large diagonal stitches, and then filling in the between areas in *Tent Stitch* in Perle 5: 809. Black beads are then added to each unit, see chart.

Woven Cross Stitch - p66 worked in the remaining 4 x 4 th squares in the lower area Perle 5: 935. Those worked down the central axis are then interlaced with two rounds of Tapestry Braid #12: 007 *(Woven Cross Stitched Laced)* but those on either side of this axis in the lower half have a *Cross Stitch* on top in Perle 5: 930.

To complete both sides, add a button to each of the central squares with a bead on top.

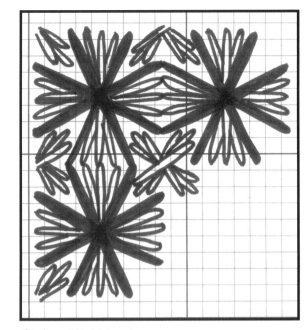

Rhodes Stitch Variation

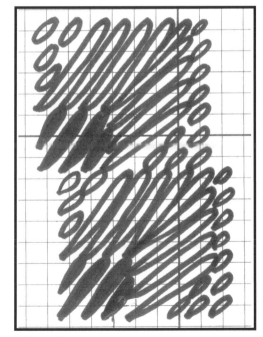

Offset Mosaic

37

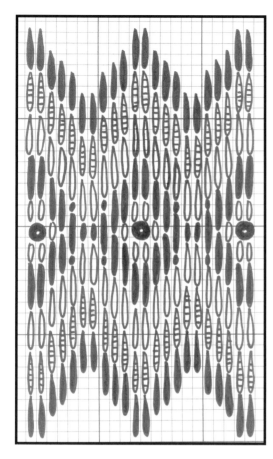

Florentine Stitch with beads

Central Gusset

Work *Florentine Stitch* with beads down the long strip starting in the centre (this becomes the centre bottom of the bag) using all colours. Do not complete the ends until the gusset is stitched to the front and back pieces of the bag as the ends will need to be finished with a straight edge. Add beads to the centre of the lozenges. (See Chart p35 for threads to use.)

Assembling the Bag

1. Trim excess canvas around bag front and back. Leave approximately 1cm (1/2") seam allowance on the sides and base but leave 24 threads of canvas on the top edges. Trim the long sides of the Florentine strip to 1cm also but at this stage *do not* trim the short ends.

2. Make a tassel (using DMC Perle 5: 310 - finished length 8cm/3in) and secure to the centre base of the Florentine Strip. (This is easier to do now rather than later when the bag is assembled). See FINISHING, AND OTHER THINGS pages 74-81.

3. Pin the Florentine gusset to the front and back, pinning from the bottom centre up each side. The Florentine patterns should match at the top edge of the bag on both sides. Stitch on a sewing machine. Complete Florentine stitching to achieve the straight edge.

4. Work a row of *Satin Stitch* over four threads of the canvas in Perle 5: 935 around the top edge of the bag, opening out and stitching through the seam allowances. On completion of the satin stitch trim excess canvas from the top edge so that only eight threads remain. Turn over four threads and work *Buttonhole Stitch* over the resulting doubled four threads in Perle 5: 310, then work *Raised Stem Band* into the front side of the *Buttonhole Stitch* until it is covered, approximately six rows, continue on the inside till covered. Work a row of *Backstitch* between the *Satin Stitch* row and the *Raised Stem Edge* in Tapestry Braid #12: 007 (see p75 for stitches).

5. Cut black cord into two and slip stitch around side seams leaving equal lengths extending beyond the top edge. Make a simple knot near the ends of each cord, pull tight, and secure with a few stitches in a black thread, cut off any excess cord flush with knot. Loosely knot all four ends together part-way down.

6. Cut out lining. Pin side seams and fit inside bag to check fitting. Adjust if necessary, then sew. Place inside bag, fold over seam allowance on top edge and slipstitch beneath Raised Stem Band on the inside of the bag.

GARDEN ROOM DECOR BAG (5)
Strong colours, butterflies and the chorus of birds...

For additional detail refer to colour photograph page 41
Finished size 12 x 15cm (5 x 6in)

Materials

One piece of White Interlock Canvas 14 tpi 20 cm x 40 cm (8" x 16")
Lining Fabric, cotton or silk, white or cream, 20 cm x 40 cm (8" x 16")
Household enamel spray paint, colour Burgundy
Alternative Canvas: Zweigart Hobby Art Canvas, Colour 954, Xmas Red

Embroidery Threads and other things:

1 skein each   DMC Cotton Perle 5: 402, 798, 830, 834, 3350
1 packet beads to match Perle 5: 3350
1.6 metres (65") satin ribbon 6mm (1/4") wide in an Avocado colour

Central tacking on canvas

To Colour your Canvas *see page 18*

Stitching *see pages 61-73*

To Begin

1. Tack centre line lengthwise over and under 4 threads (ths).
2. Start the centre panel, 8cm (3") down from the top of the canvas (this allows room for a border around the top edge of the bag and finishing).
3. Follow chart for colour placement. Stitches and threads to use are given in the text.

The chart gives only one side of the bag and will need to be continued in reverse to complete.

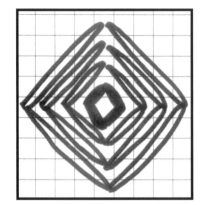

Cushion Stitch Variation # 1

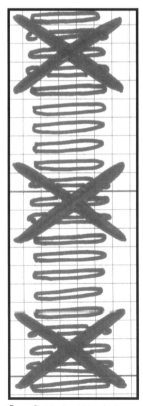

Row 8 Satin Stitch Crossed

Row 1	**Centre Panel** **(a) Cross Stitch - p66**	Perle 5: 3350, over 2 ths; 2 zigzag rows to establish 12 diamond units (refer chart). The top cross (centre) is a part cross stitch.
	(b) Cushion Stitch Variation # 1	Perle 5: 830 with 834 in centre
	(c) Vee Stitch - p70	Perle 5: 798 outer stitches, inside 402
Row 2	**Tent Stitch - p71**	Perle 5: 830 Single row worked vertically
Row 3	**Satin Stitch couched over Ribbon - p62**	Cut 4 lengths of ribbon, each 40cm (16") long, place one length next to the *Tent Stitch* row on the left side of the centre panel extend ends beyond the top edge to allow for the border plus construction of the bag. *Satin Stitch* in Perle 5: 3350 over the ribbon and 4 ths of the canvas (omitting every second stitch).
Row 4	**Tent Stitch**	Perle 5: 830 Single row worked vertically

Leave 6 ths of the canvas for Row 8

Rows 5 - 7	**Repeat Rows 2,3 and 4**	
Row 8	**Satin Stitch Crossed**	Between the ribbons work *Satin Stitch* using Perle 5: 834, over central 4 ths. Next work a Cross Stitch over the Satin with Perle 5: 798, 6 ths wide and 4 ths deep. Place beads each side of the *Cross Stitch*.

Leave a gap of 4 ths in between each *Cross Stitch* except for in the middle area which will become the bottom of the bag where a gap of 8 ths is left.

Row 9	**Milanese Straight Split - p64**	Work along each side, total width 10 ths. Outside edges Perle 5: 3350, centres Perle 5: 402 and 834, with Perle 5: 798 as a single stitch at the top. Reverse stitch sequence at the middle (base line) so that the stitch points upwards on both sides.

Repeat for the right hand side of the Décor Bag.

• Each square on this chart represents one thread of fabric

key

DMC Perle 5: 3350
DMC Perle 5: 798

DMC Perle 5: 402
DMC Perle 5: 834
DMC Perle 5: 830

Row 9
Row 6
Row 7
Row 5
Row 8
Row 4
Row 3
Row 2
Centre panel start at top

Garden Room Décor Bag 5

notes

Top Border

Refer to chart for colours to complete the top border, using Satin Stitch, Satin Stitch Crossed, Tent Stitch and Cushion Stitch.

Assembling the Bag

1. Trim sides of bag, leaving six threads of the canvas as seam allowance. Trim top edges leaving eight threads of the canvas.

2. With right sides together fold bag at base line and, matching stitch patterns, machine stitch side seams as close as possible to the stitch patterns.

3. Nick seam allowance at base, fold and slip stitch each seam allowance back to wrong side of embroidery.

4. Turn over eight threads at the top edge of the bag and slip stitch to the inside. Stitch ends of ribbon to the inside of the bag but leave a 1 cm (1/2") loop above the top edge to thread the hanging cords through.

5. *Side Cords and Tassels* - There are four side cords in total, two each side with a finished length of 15 cm (6") made using Perle 5: 834. Make four tassels by wrapping Perle 5: 3350 20 times around a 6cm (2 1/2") card. Secure tassels in centre fold of cord. See FINISHINGS, AND OTHER THINGS pages 74-81 for more information on making cords and tassels and securing tassels on to the twisted cord.

6. *Hanging Cord or Handles:* Make two cords with a finished length of 35cm (14") using Perle 5: 834. Place a knotted end of cord at the centre front of the bag and thread the cord through the two ribbon loops on the right, then loop the cord over to the other side and bring the cord through the ribbon loops on the other side of the front back to the centre. Secure knots inside bag. Make a second cord and thread it through the other side of the bag in the same way.

7. Cut fabric lining 14 x 32cm (5 1/2 x 13"), sew side seams. Place inside bag, fold under top edge and blind stitch inside the top edge of the bag.

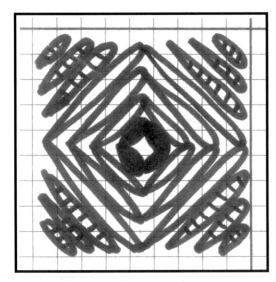

Cushion Stitch - used in top border

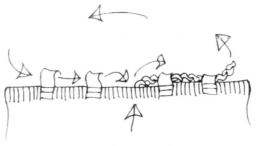

Threading top cord

DRAWING ROOM DECOR BAG (6)
Finery, family treasures and cucumber sandwiches...

For additional reference refer to colour photograph page 44.
Finished size 12 x 18cm (4 3/4 x 7in)

Materials

One piece of White Interlock Canvas 14 tpi 25 cm x 35 cm (10" x 14")
Lining Fabric, cotton or silk, white or cream, 25 cm x 35 cm (10" x 14")
Polysol Transfer Paints: Yellow with a touch of Black
                                 Violet
Alternative Canvas: Zweigart Hobby Art Canvas, Colour 235, Yellow

Embroidery Threads and other things:

1 skein each DMC Cotton Perle 5: 834 and 3041
3 skeins DMC Cotton Perle 5: 783
1 skein Kreinik Metallic Tapestry Braid #12: 002J
2 cards Neon Rays Needlepoint Ribbon: Deep Gold
1 packet 3mm Butterick Beads 0124 / 10071D Gold
50cm (20") gold chain

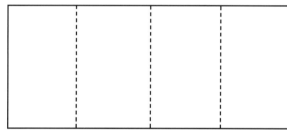

tacking on canvas

To Colour the Canvas **See page 16**

Stitching **See page 61-73**

To Begin:

1. With the canvas placed horizontally, tack a line through the centre and then tack a further centre line in each half. The front and back are the same.
2. Start in the centre of one half approximately 3cm (1 1/2") from the bottom of the canvas - at the Diamond Point.
3. Follow chart for colour placement. Stitches and threads to use are given in the text.

The chart gives only one side of the bag repeat for the second side.

key

DMC Perle 5: 783

DMC Perle 5: 834

Neon Rays Needlepoint Ribbon – Deep Gold

Kreinik Metallic Tapestry Braid #12: 002J

DMC Perle 5: 3041

Central Band   Side Panel

Mosaic Stitch.

Diagonal Satin Stitch – outside edge.

Jacquard Stitch.

Building Blocks.

Milanese stitch.

Start here

• **Each square on this chart represents one thread of fabric**

Drawing Room Décor Bag 6

The Diamond Point

Upright Cross - p66

Work *Upright Cross Stitches* over 2 threads(ths) to form the outside row of a diamond using Kreinik Metallic Tapestry Braid #12: 002J.

Double Cross - p66

With the same thread work a *Double Cross Stitch* in the centre of this Diamond.

Cross Stitch - p66

Work Cross Stitch to fill the shape alternating Perle 5: 3041 and 834.

Central Band: *This band is 22 ths wide and worked from the left:*

Satin Stitch - p63

Worked over 3 ths on each outside edge of this band using the gold Needlepoint Ribbon (refer page 62 for additional information on stitching with ribbon). The first stitch is only over 2 ths to accommodate the diamond Cross Stitched shape.

Woven Satin Stitch - p63

Work in the central area using Kreinik Metallic Tapestry Braid #12: 002J and Perle 5: 834 for the vertical stitching (with the centre row having three vertical rows instead of two), and Perle 5: 783 for the horizontal stitches. Fit the stitch pattern around the diamond shape at the base.

Side Panels: *Worked from the base up, right side first reverse for left, 24 ths wide*

Milanese Stitch on the Diagonal - p73

Keeping to the diagonal edge established by the diamond, work *Milanese Stitch on the Diagonal* in Perle 5: 3041, the first stitch is a part-unit, followed by 11 full units.

Building Blocks - p73

Above the *Milanese Stitch on the Diagonal* work *Building Blocks* using Perle 5: 834 and 783 to form side triangle shape.

Using Perle 5: 783 work a series of irregular Diagonal Satin Stitches on the lower side of the *Milanese Stitch on the Diagonal* and between the Building Blocks row above. (Refer to chart.)

notes

notes

Jacquard Stitch - p73

Work a Tent Stitch row in Perle 5: 3041. Then a row of Diagonal Satin Stitch over 3 ths using the Needlepoint Ribbon; then a row of Tent Stitch in Kreinik Tapestry Braid #12: 002J, followed by another row of Diagonal Satin Stitch over 3 ths using Needlepoint Ribbon then a Tent Stitch row in Perle 5: 3041.

Diagonal Satin Stitch

Along the remaining very outside edge to the top of the bag work two rows of Diagonal Satin Stitch each over 2 ths using the Needlepoint Ribbon for the outside edge and Kreinik Tapestry Braid #12: 002J for the inside edge. Each row to slant in the opposite direction to the other.

Mosaic Stitch Variation #2

In the remaining space, work Mosaic Stitch Variation 2 using Perle 5: 783 for the three long stitches, then Perle 5: 3041 with Kreinik Tapestry Braid #12: 002J for the center stitches - this combination creates an overall zigzag or diamond pattern.

Stitch beads down through the central panel as shown and also around the diamond shape.

Assembling the Bag

1. Cut out stitched pieces, leaving six threads on the sides, the equivalent on the diagonal sides, and eight threads along the top edges.

2. Make the eight smaller tassels in Perle 5: 783 with a finished length of 3cm (1 1/4") and the larger tassel (finished length 7cm (2 3/4") in all the colours including the ribbon (see FINISHINGS, AND OTHER THINGS pages 74-81). All the small tassels are attached to a short twisted cord loop made with the Perle 5: 783 (make a twisted cord 50 cm (20") long), using four threads secure and cut into 8 sections (see p47), while the large tassel has a loop of gold chain 5 cm (2") cut off the 50 cm (20") length. Attach these to the seam allowance of the right side of one half of the bag (see diagram for positioning) and stitch firmly in place.

3. Place the right sides of the two stitched panels together, making sure that tassels are clear of the seam. Stitch side seams on the machine (do not stitch over the point where the gold chain of the larger tassel is placed otherwise you will break your machine needle!!!). Turn bag.

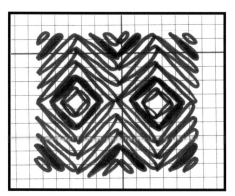

Mosaic Stitch Variation #2

4. Stitch and secure the chain ends on to the seam allowances, inside the bag.

5. Turn over four of the eight threads left around the top, and work *Buttonhole Stitch* in Perle 5: 783 over this edge, then work *Raised Stem Band* over the buttonhole stitch on the outside (approx. 6 rows) and inside of the bag in the same colour (see p75 for stitches).

6. Cut two pieces of lining fabric to match the bag shape, stitch side seams. Place inside bag, turn over top edge and slip stitch to the base of the *Raised Stem Band*.

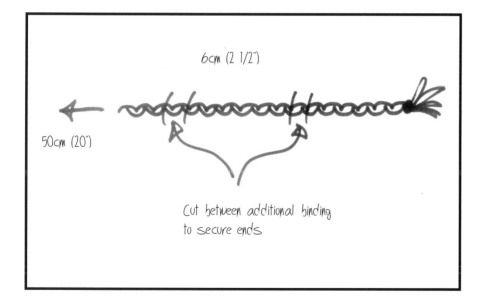

6cm (2 1/2")

50cm (20")

Cut between additional binding
to secure ends

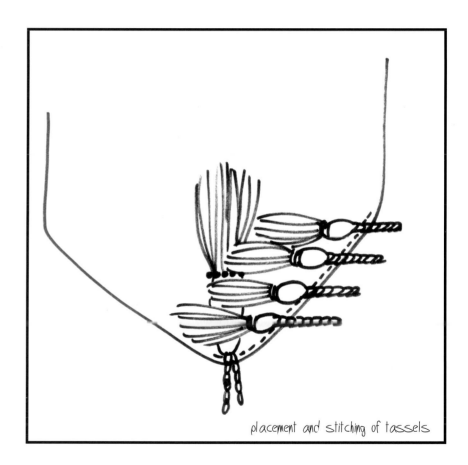

placement and stitching of tassels

Lobby Room Décor Bag 7

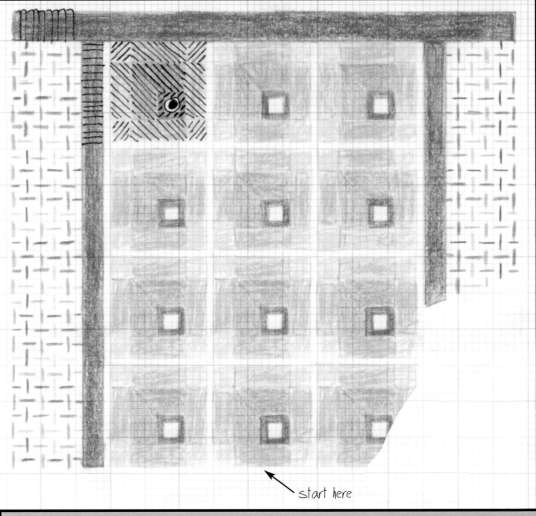

start here

• Each square on this chart represents one thread of fabric

key

DMC Perle 5: 834

DMC Perle 5: 3348

DMC Perle 5: 402

DMC Perle 5: 554

DMC Perle 5: 745

LOBBY ROOM DÉCOR BAG 7
Arrivals, departures and journeys...

For additional detail refer to colour photograph on page 48.
Finished size 13 x 11cm (5 x 4 1/4")

This Décor Bag is worked on an unpainted canvas with light coloured threads. The thread colours are deliberately pale making the contrast between the white canvas and the stitching understated and subtle.

Materials

One piece of White Interlock Canvas 14 threads per inch (tpi) 20cm x 30 cm (8ins x 12ins)
Lining Fabric, cotton or silk, white, cream or to match one of the threads 20 cm x 30 cm (8 x 12 ins)
(I used lilac)

Embroidery Threads and other things:

1 skein each DMC Cotton Perle 5: 402, 554, 745, 834,& 3348
24 x 4mm beads (I used green) with a further 24 size 11 beads in a contrast colour (I used orange).

central tacking on canvas

Stitching *see pages 61-73*

To Begin

1. Take a tacking thread over and under four threads through the centre of the canvas, in both directions. The front and back of the bag are the same.
2. The centre grid is made up of twelve Composite Cushion Blocks on each side, three wide and four deep. Start at what will be the bottom edge, the horizontal tacked centre line, and centre the middle block over the vertical central tacking line.
3. Follow the chart for colour placement. Stitches and threads to use are given in the text.

The chart gives only one side of the bag and will need to be continued to complete the bag.

notes

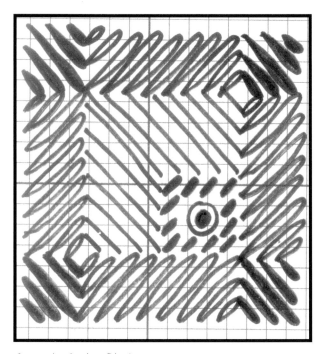

Composite Cushion Block

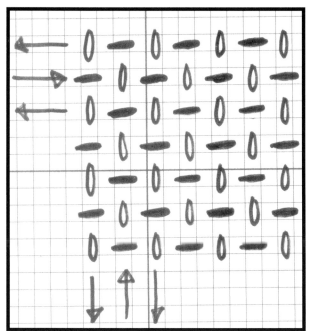

Pattern Darning

Composite Cushion Blocks

Use Perle 5: 745 for the corner squares, Perle 5: 3348 for the outside edges, Perle 5: 834 and 402 for the inside diagonals, and Perle 5: 554 for the *Tent Stitch* squares.

Inside this corner square is a green bead with a smaller contrasting orange turning bead (or bead colours of your choice). Continue working all 12 of these blocks leaving a single thread of canvas showing between each block. Repeat for the reverse side of the bag.

Satin Stitch - p63

The *Satin Stitch* borders are worked over 3 threads (ths) of the canvas in Perle 5: 554 with a single thread of canvas between the Satin Stitch and the *Composite Cushion Blocks.*

Pattern Darning

The outside borders are worked in *Pattern Darning* running stitch over and under 2 ths of the canvas. Work each of the rows in different colours but at this stage stitch the vertical rows only, as the horizontal rows are worked after the side seams are stitched.

Assembling the Bag, Cord and Tassels

1. Trim the canvas leaving six threads as a seam allowance on the sides of the bag and eight threads on the top edge.

2. With right sides together fold bag at base line and stitch side seams.

3. Nick seam allowance at base fold and slip stitch each seam allowance back to wrong side of embroidery.

4. Turn back to right side and work the horizontal *Pattern Darning* rows across the outside borders and side seams.

5. Turn over four threads at the top edge of the bag and work *Buttonhole Stitch* in Perle 5: 554 over the two layers. Then work *Raised Stem Band* (same colour) in the front side of the *Buttonhole Stitch* until it is covered, approximately six rows, then continue over on the inside until covered (see p75 for stitches).

6. *Side Tassels:* Make six, small, individual tassels for each side with a finished length of 4cm (1 1/2 in), using one thread of each of the colours. Attach them at evenly spaced intervals by stitching through the side seams and secure each firmly with a couple of stitches near the top. Trim all ends to equal lengths.

7. *Cord:* Make two twisted cords, using all the threads, for handles. The cords have a finished length of 35cm (14in.) (see FINISHINGS, AND OTHER THINGS pages 74-81). They are tucked inside the lining approximately 2.5cm (1in.) in from the side seams front and back.

8. Cut a piece of lining fabric to fit inside the bag, sew side seams. Place inside bag, fold under top edge and blind stitch to the base of the *Buttonhole Stitch* on the inside.

notes

lobby room

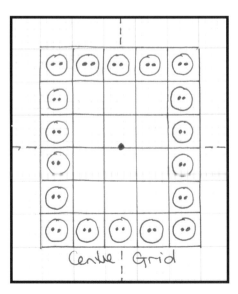

NURSERY ROOM DÉCOR BAG

New beginnings, boy or girl, lots of joy…

For additional detail refer to colour photograph on page 54.
Finished size 16 x 14cm (6 1/4 x 5 1/2")

Materials

One piece of White Interlock Canvas 14 threads per inch (tpi) 20 x 35 cm (8 x 14 ins)
Lining Fabric, cotton or silk, white, cream or to match one of the threads, 20 x 35 cm (8 x 14 ins)

Embroidery Threads and other things:

1 skein each DMC Cotton Perle 5: 340, 598, 745, 951, & 954
2 skeins DMC Cotton Perle 5: 754
44 Peach coloured buttons 12mm diameter (112 ins diameter)
2 metres (2 1/4 yds) satin ribbon in teal (to match Perle 5: 598)
2.5 metres (2 3/4 yds) satin ribbon in lilac (to match Perle 5: 340)
Lemon or yellow beads, approximately 40 size 11

Stitching   see pages 61-73

To Begin

1. Stitch a tacking thread over and under four threads through the centre of the canvas in both directions, then tack a further centre line in each half. This will give a centre point for each side of the Decor Bag.
2. Follow the chart for colour placement. Stitches and threads to use are given in the text.
3. The arrows indicate the centre.

This chart gives one side of the bag, the front and back are the same.

Central Rectangular Grid.

Tent Stitch - p71

Starting at the centre work one Tent Stitch in Perle 5: 951 then work a further 20 Tent Stitches to the left and the same number to the right (41 in total). Continue in Tent Stitch following the chart to create the grid into which the different patterns are placed.

Tent Stitch

On the inner 12 squares (see chart) work tent stitch in Perle 5: 340.

Cross Stitches - p66

Work four cross stitches over 2 threads (ths) in each square in Perle 5: 754. Weave Perle 5: 954 through the four cross stitches, making two journeys. Place a lemon/yellow bead in the centre of each ring.

Diagonal Stitches

The outside series of squares (18 in total) have two diagonal stitches at their inside corners using Perle 5: 745. A button is stitched into these squares using Perle 5: 954 however, this is best postponed until all the remaining stitching is completed otherwise your stitching thread may get caught up in the buttons.

Tent Stitch over Diagonal Couching

The diagonal corners are worked in rows using Perle 5: 754 and 745 alternatively.

Satin Stitch couching over ribbon - p62

The side panels are worked from the inside edge to the outside edge. The satin stitch is over 4 ths with the ribbon centred beneath, note how the satin stitch is 'staggered'.
Rows 1 & 5: Lilac ribbon couched with Perle 5: 598
Rows 2 & 4: Teal ribbon couched with Perle 5: 754
Row 3: Lilac ribbon couched with Perle 5: 954.

Assembling the Bag, Cord and Tassels

1. Cut out stitched pieces, leaving approximately six threads on the straight sides and the equivalent on the diagonal edges.

2. With right sides together machine stitch sides and lower edge together (do not stitch top edge or top diagonals). Slipstitch seam allowances back on to the wrong side of the stitching.

3. Make the six tassels in Perle 5: 754, with a finished length of 3cm (1 1/4 in). To finish add a yellow bead, a peach coloured button then a second yellow bead on before stitching the tassels to the appropriate corners. For more information on cords and tassels see FINISHINGS AND OTHER THINGS pages 74-81.

4. Twist a cord from the remaining Perle 5: 754 using eight threads and from this cut two 6 cm (2 1/2 ins) lengths (oversew about-to-be cut ends of the cord to stop it unraveling) and form a loop on opposite sides of the top edge and match with buttons on the other sides. Attach longer cord ends at side seams.

5. Cut out two lining pieces from lining fabric and sew side and lower. seams. Place inside bag and fold in seam allowances around the top edge and slip stitch.

notes

Tent Stitch over Diagonal Couching

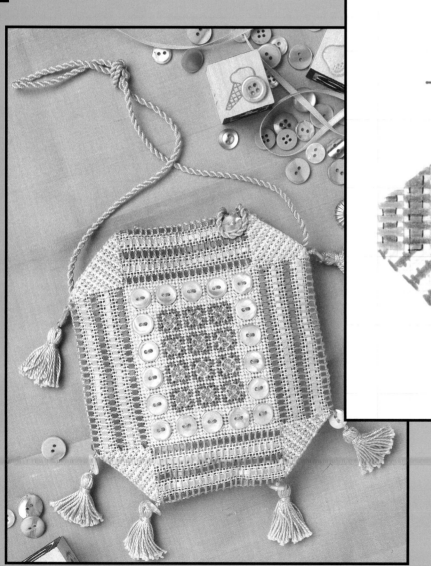

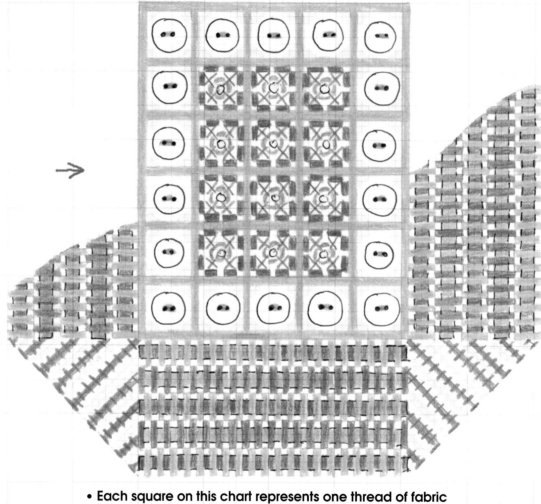

• Each square on this chart represents one thread of fabric

DMC Perle 5: 745

DMC Perle 5: 951

DMC Perle 5: 754

DMC Perle 5: 598 + teal ribbon

DMC Perle 5: 340 + lilac ribbon

DMC Perle 5: 954

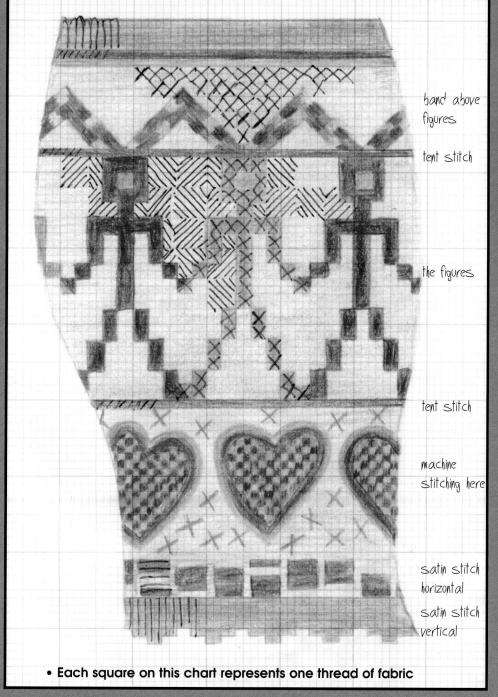

band above figures

tent stitch

the figures

tent stitch

machine stitching here

satin stitch horizontal

satin stitch vertical

• **Each square on this chart represents one thread of fabric**

Aztec Décor Bag 9

Kreinik Tapestry #12 002

Hand-dyed hues: 508

DMC Perle 5: 977

DMC Perle 5: 355

DMC Perle 5: 552

notes

Aztec Décor Bag 9

Worship, ritual and treasure...

For additional detail refer to colour photograph on page 55
Finished size height 16cm (6 1/2in)

Materials

One piece of White Interlock Canvas 14 threads per inch (tpi) 15 x 30cm (6" x 12")
Lining Fabric, cotton or silk, in a colour to match, or paint with silk paints to co-ordinate 25 x 30cm (10" x 12")
DEKA Silk Textile Paints, Outliner: Gold
Alternative Canvas: Zweigart Hobby Art Canvas, Colour 235, Yellow

Embroidery Treads and Other Things:

1 skein each	DMC Cotton Perle 5: 355, 552
2 skeins	DMC Cotton Perle: 977
1 skein	Hand-dyed Hues Variegated Thread Perle 5: 508 (shades of deep gold, pink and purple)
1 reel	Kreinik Tapestry Braid #12: 002
1 reel	Gold sewing thread to match Kreinik Tapestry Braid #12: 002
1 reel	Variegated rayon machine sewing thread, gold and wine red combination

Collection of small feathers 1 - 1.5cm (1/2") in length
50 x 3 mm Beads in red, brown, mustard colours and small purple beads for turning

To Colour your Canvas *see page 15*

Stitching *see pages 61-73*

To Begin

1. Follow the chart for colour placement. Stitches and threads to use are given in the text.

The chart gives a section of the design only, the completed design has ten figures in total, continue to complete required area.

Machine Stitched Area

Measure approximately 9cm (4 ins) down from a long horizontal edge of the canvas and using the rayon machine threads and your sewing machine, stitch a band 20 threads (ths) (3cm or 1 1/4ins) wide with repeated rows of machine stitching. This will eventually get covered with the heart shapes (see illustration).

machine stitched band on canvas

Tent Stitch

On the top edge of the machine stitched band, work a single row of *Tent Stitch* in Perle 5: 552, then leave a space of 32 ths above this row and work another row of Tent Stitch in the same colour. The space in between is for the figure shapes.

The Figures

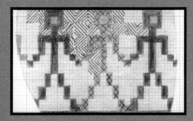

These are worked in *Cross Stitch* - p66 over 2 ths (see chart). There are 10 in total, alternating with colours Perle 5:977 and 355. They are holding hands and feet and the *Cross Stitch* at these points is worked with one diagonal in one colour and the other diagonal in the other. The square in the middle of the heads is *Cross Stitch* using Kreinik Tapestry #12: 002.

Background area around the figures

This area is worked in the rayon machine thread in alternating *Cushion Stitch* - p72 over 4 ths. The smaller spaces around the figures are stitched keeping the pattern correct.

Band above the figures

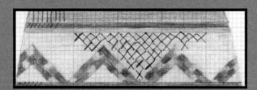

This area is 13 ths wide. There are 2 zigzag rows of *Satin Stitch* each over 2 ths using Hand-dyed Hues Variegated Thread: 508. These are centred above the heads in the section below. *Cross Stitches* over 2 ths are worked in the machine rayon thread above the zigzags. The last two rows (over the 12th and 13th threads) are a couched thread of Kreinik Tapestry #12: 002 stitched down with the gold sewing thread, followed by another row of *Tent Stitch* in Perle 5: 552 over the thirteenth thread.

these need not be all the same or symmetrical

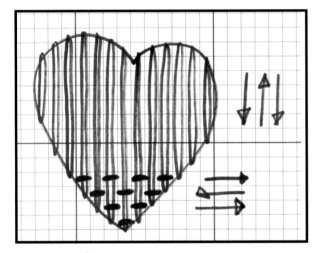

hearts in surface weaving

Machine Stitched Band

Six heart shapes are evenly placed along this band (use template). Couch the outline of the heart shapes using 3 ths of Perle 5: 552 stitched down with the Hand-dyed Hues Thread Perle 5: 508. The shapes are then outlined with Kreinik Tapestry #12: 002 couched in place with gold sewing thread. The spaces inside the hearts are covered with *Surface Weaving* using Perle 5: 977 and 355. Freely stitched *Cross Stitches* in Perle 5: 977 are then scattered in between the hearts.

Satin Stitch - p63

Underneath the hearts, stitch bands of five horizontal satin stitches over 4 ths leaving one thread in between. They are stitched using Hand-dyed Hues Variegated Thread Perle 5: 508.

Satin Stitch

The final row of satin stitch is worked vertically over 6 ths using Perle 5: 977. However, so that this bottom edge does not become too bulky to gather into the base, the lower edge of the *Satin Stitch* is zigzagged to accommodate the tucks (see chart). The top edge of the *Satin Stitch* remains straight.

Beads and Feathers

To complete add a string of three, 3mm beads at the base of each heart (use the small purple beads for turning). Trim the top of the figures by poking some feathers through the canvas above the head of each figure, finishing with a 3mm bead, selecting the beads randomly. (Refer to the photograph p55 for additional detail.)

Assembling the Bag and Cord

1. Trim top edge of canvas leaving eight threads of the canvas. Trim the sides and bottom edge of the bag, leaving six threads of the canvas as seam allowance.

2. Fold bag with right sides together, matching stitch patterns and machine stitch side seam as close as possible to stitch patterns. Slip stitch each seam allowance back to wrong side of embroidery.

3. Turn over four threads at the top edge of the bag and work *Buttonhole Stitch* in Perle 5: 977 over the two layers. Then work *Raised Stem Band* (same colour) on the front side of the *Buttonhole Stitch* until it is covered, approximately six rows, continue on the inside until it is also covered (see p75 for stitches).

4. Make a 5cm (2ins) diameter, firm cardboard disc. With the cardboard disc as a template cut a circle from the lining fabric but add a 1cm (1/2") seam allowance. Place a running stitch in the seam allowance, pull up with the cardboard disc inside and secure firmly.

5. Manipulate the base so that the disc fits comfortably on to the base of the bag. Secure with stitching, then cover with a twisted cord made using Perle 5: 977.

6. For the lining make a similar but longer bag from the lining fabric with the top edge channel stitched. The lining extends approximately 5cm (2ins) above the canvas bag when completed.

7. Make two twisted cords each with a finished length of 50cm (20") using Perle 5: 977 and Kreinik Tapestry #12: 002. Thread through the channel at the top edge of the lining in draw-string fashion (one cord emerging from each side of the bag). Knot cords together. Make two tassels using the same threads with a finished length of 5cm (2"). Note this tassel was folded over the knotted ends of the drawstring cord and the head has been decorated with detached buttonhole stitching. All around the base of the detached buttonhole stitching brown 3mm beads have been attached with a purple turning bead. Refer to the colour photograph page 55.

See FINISHINGS, AND OTHER THINGS pages 74-81 for more information on making cords and tassels and securing tassels on to the twisted cord.

notes

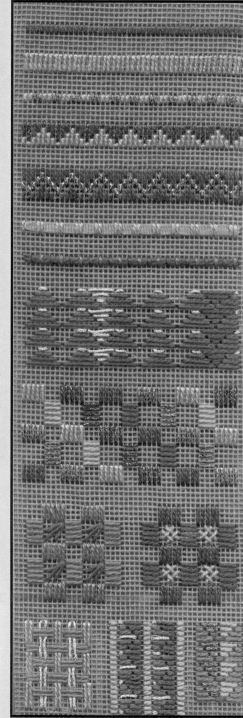

far left - sampler of straight stitches
centre and above - samplers of cross stitches

STITCHES
On all stitch diagrams each line represents one thread.

Stitch Journeys:

The charts in this book do not have any stitch directions. Most may be achieved by working in any number of sequences and as long as the stitch looks correct on the right side, the reverse side can take care of itself - lets face it, with DECOR BAGS as in most needlepoint articles, the reverse side is eventually lined. The stitch titles *italicised* in the instructions for each bag will be found in the STITCH CHARTS pages 61-73. Also on these charts there is a reference number for each bag where the stitch is used e.g. 1. Morning Room Decor Bag, 2. Mediterranean Room Decor Bag, etc.

Stitch Movements:

When making the stitches it is always best to work them in two movements i.e. bring the complete thread through from the reverse side of the canvas, then take it down through to the back again pulling the thread firmly so that the stitch sits comfortably on the canvas. Do not attempt to go down and up through the canvas at the same time as this may distort the canvas. Working needlepoint in a frame eliminates any attempts at this and working each stitch with two movements soon becomes a good habit.

Counting on the diagonal:

Some stitches e.g. Diamond Eyelets, Blackberry Stitch, Cushion Stitch etc require making a diagonal journey on the canvas. Eventually your eye will begin to read the canvas on the diagonal but until it does, count the canvas threads out on a horizontal line first, then the same number vertically. You will then reach the diagonal point.

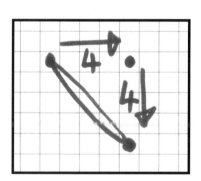

And working on the diagonal:

Any diagonal stitches will tend to distort and twist the canvas even if you stitch with a loose tension. If you are planning a DECOR BAG with lots of diagonal stitches, I would strongly advise securing the canvas into a frame to keep it square. Even better still, select straight stitches in amongst your diagonal stitches to control any twisting. If working large areas of Tent Stitch, particularly in one colour, you may wish to work it on the diagonal **(also known as Basketweave/Continental or Diagonal Tent Stitch).** However, DECOR BAGS are all about different stitch patterns so blocks of Tent Stitch are not likely.

your stitches

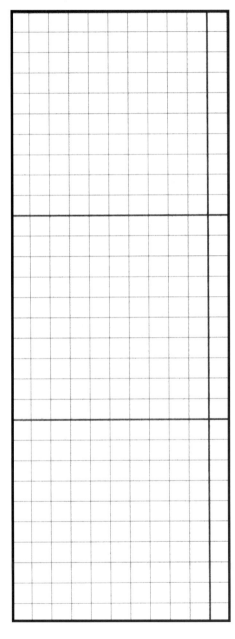

Starting and Finishing:

Stitching is always started with a waste knot on the end of the thread. The thread is taken through the canvas approximately 4cm (1 1/2") away from where the stitching is to commence and subsequent stitching covers the excess thread now lying on the back of the canvas. The waste knot is cut off when reached with the stitching. As your bag develops, new threads may be worked into the back of a previously stitched area when starting. At the completion of each thread, the short length left may be worked back through some of the stitching on the reverse of the canvas and any excess trimmed away.

STITCH CHARTS

Straight stitches

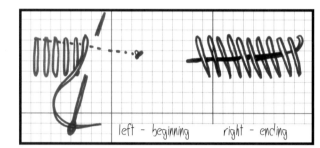

left - beginning   right - ending

Satin Stitch Variations:

When working any of the satin stitch patterns, always remember to take the thread right around the canvas - if you come up on the top line, go down on the bottom line and back up again on the top line. The front side will give a straight vertical stitch and the reverse side will have a slightly slanted stitch. (See illustration for Starting and Finishing above where the stitch used is Satin Stitch.

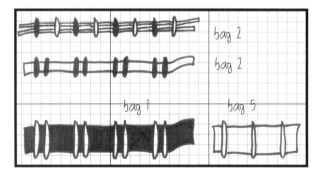

bag 2
bag 2
bag 1   bag 5

Satin stitch couching over thread and ribbons

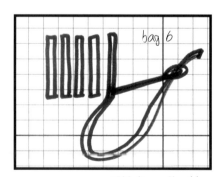

bag 6

Stitching with ribbon:

There are some lovely rayon and silk ribbons on the market these days which may be used as thread when stitching your DECOR BAG (see Drawing Room Decor Bag). The ribbon is inclined to twist when stitching so to avoid this, stitch through the ribbon as you take your needle through to the over side of the canvas. Your ribbon should now lie flat in its stitch.

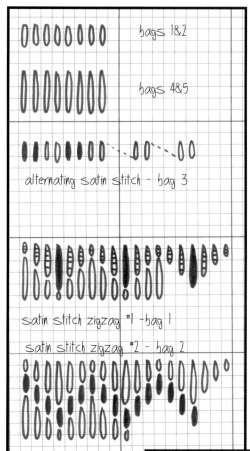

bags 1&2

bags 4&5

alternating satin stitch - bag 3

satin stitch zigzag #1 - bag 1

satin stitch zigzag #2 - bag 2

satin stitch

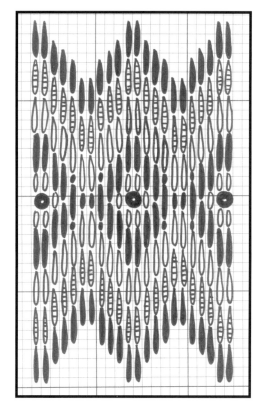

Florentine stitch with beads - bag 4

Florentine stitch with eyelets - bag 3

satin stitch - woven - bag 6

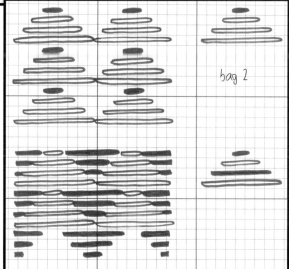

bag 2

Milanese straight stitch

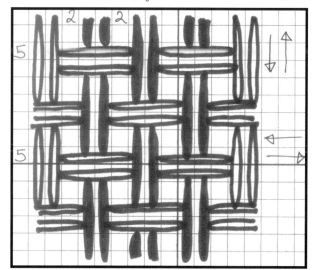

63

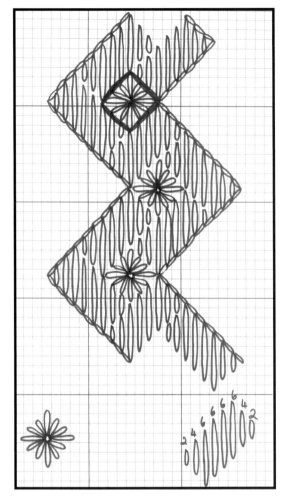

satin stitch, eyelets and back
stitch - bag 2

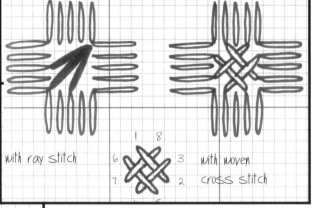

with ray stitch

	1	8	
6			3
7			2
		5	

with woven
cross stitch

satin stitch blocks alternating - bag 4

satin stitch blocks alternating - bag 4

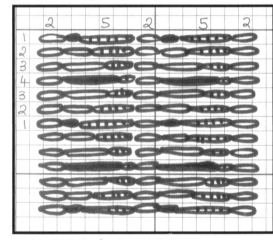

satin stitch border horizontal

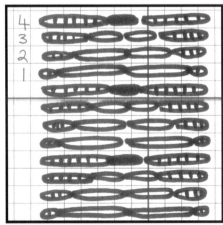

Milanese straight stitch split - bag 5

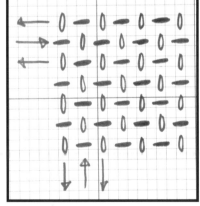

pattern darning - bag 7

weaving stitch - bags 3 & 9

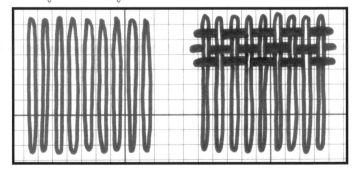

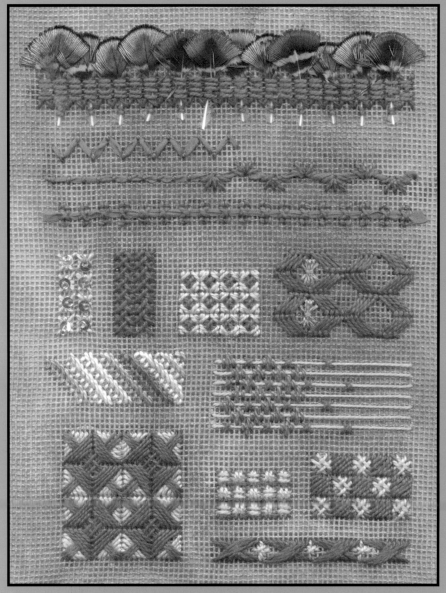

above - sampler of feathers and mixed stitches
centre - sampler of diagonal stitches
far right - sampler of straight stitches

Cross stitches

Cross Stitches:

Everyone can do a Cross Stitch!!! Whatever sequence you use to achieve it just make sure the top cross is always going in the same direction for subsequent cross stitches.

cross stitch
- bags 1, 5 & 8

upright cross
- bags 3 & 6

combined cross &
upright cross - bag 6

cross stitch - woven - bag 4
take thread under bar when completing 7-8

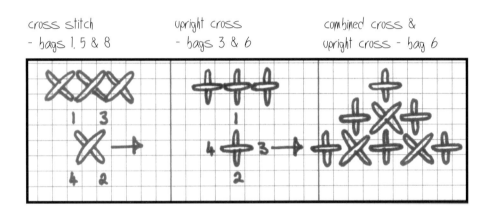

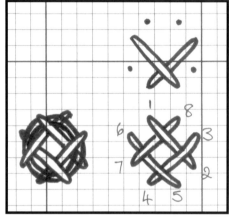

diamond eyelet & half Rhodes stitch
- bag 3

double cross
- bags 1 & 6

rice stitch

rice stitch variation

blackberry stitch - bag 2

satin stitch crossed
- bag 5

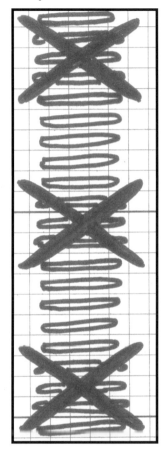

Rhodes stitch variation with
Rhodes cross stitch in
between

Rhodes cross stitch - bag 4

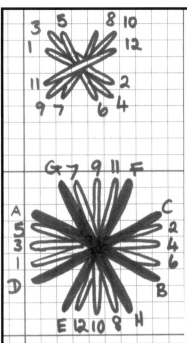

3 5 8 10
1 12
11 2
9 7 6 4

G 7 9 11 F
A C
5 2
3 4
1 6
D B
E 12 10 8 H

Rhodes stitch
variation

woven cross stitch combination - bag 3

cross stitch

large double
diagonal cross
stitch

double upright
cross stitch

interlaced
circles

side
straight
stitches

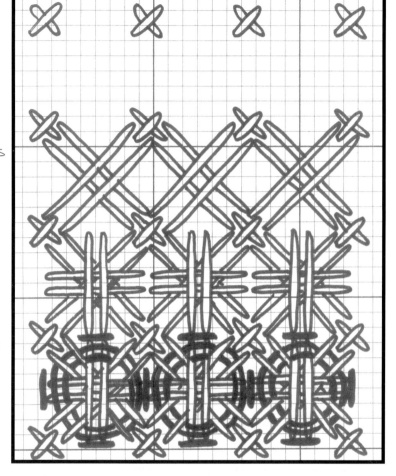

67

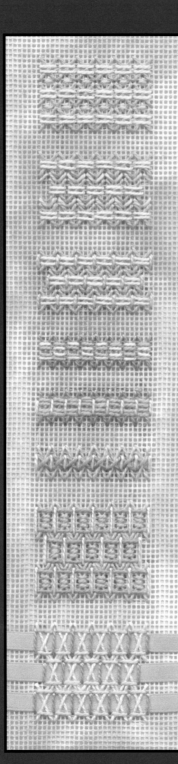

far left - sampler
mixed stitches

centre - oblong
crosses with satin
stitches

right - cushion stitch
sampler

Mixed stitches

Sheaf Stitches:

These are made from Satin Stitches bunched together with a small horizontal stitch. This small stitch starts under the Satin Stitch threads and is best achieved with three movements, one to bring the thread up between the threads, then the second to slide it under to the left. It is then quite easy to push the Satin Stitches aside from the front, when going down through to the back of the canvas on the right.

sheaf stitch

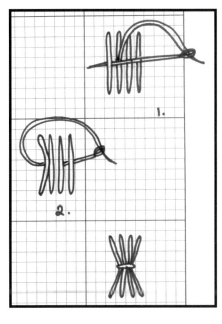

sheaf stitch variation #1 - bag 1
over 4 ths every third stitch worked twice

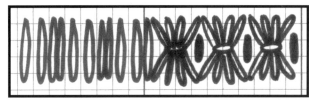

sheaf stitch variation #2 - bag 2
over 6 ths, single straight stitch
over 2 ths in gaps

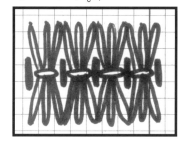

sheaf stitch variation #3 - bag 3
over 4 ths with straight stitch filler

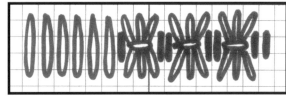

offset mosaic - bag 4

chain stitch filling with
backstitch between rows

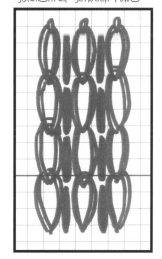

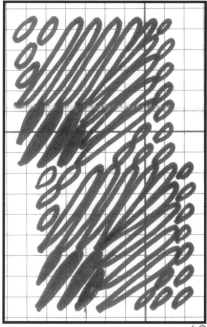

chain stitch - canvas work variation
stitched backwards

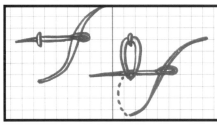

buttonhole half rounds and upright cross - bag 3

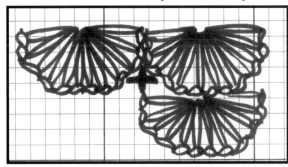

chain stitch long legged woven

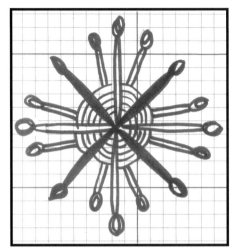

1. sets of 3 long legged chain stitches
2. add diagonal long legged chain stitches
3. weave centre

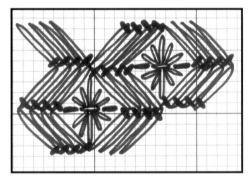

diagonal tied composite stitch - bag 2
1. diagonal tied stitch - see p26
2. sheaf stitch
3. horizontal straight stitch

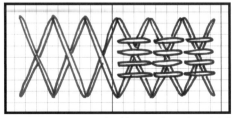

cross stitch oblong with satin stitch

Vee stitch - bag 5

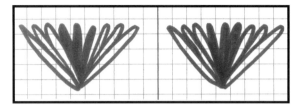

encroaching herringbone

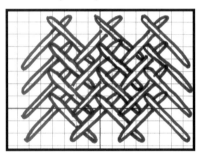

back stitch - ringed - pull tight to create holes in canvas

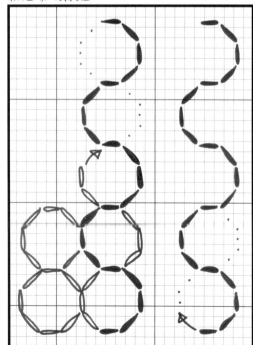

feather secured over cross stitch under satin stitch

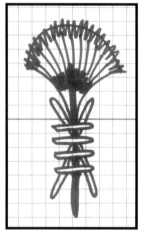

cross stitch

woven wheels

lacing between diagonally placed cross stitch

beads or French knots

further lacing

buttonhole detached

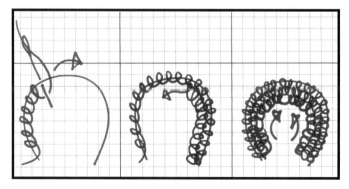

Diagonal stitches

Tent Stitch (or Petit Point):

The smallest of all needlepoint stitches and needlepoint's origin. It is worked across one diagonal intersection of the canvas, either vertically or horizontally. To work 'true' Tent Stitch go back over one thread of the canvas and forward two threads, making a longer stitch on the reverse of the work than on the front.

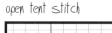
open tent stitch

tent stitch worked horizontally - bags 1, 4, 5, 6, 7, 8 & 9

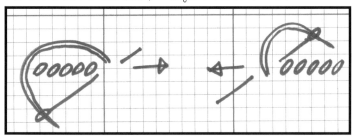

tent stitch worked diagonally

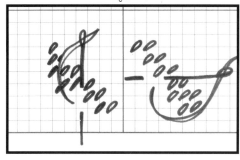

tent stitch worked vertically

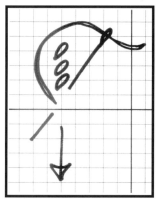

Eyelets:

Square, Diamond, any type of Eyelet, is always fun to do and make great focal points and texture. Always remember to come up on the outside edge of your Eyelet and go down through the middle hole, pulling your thread taut so as to enlarge the hole. Always work repeat Eyelets in the same direction e.g. clockwise, to achieve a neat look; and do not drag thread across behind a hole, it often needs to be secured elsewhere on the reverse of the work before moving to the next stitch.

eyelet diamond variation #1 with contrast stitches

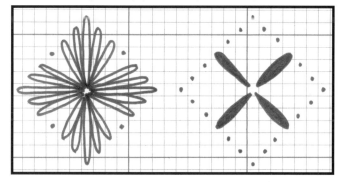

eyelet square

eyelet diamond - bag 3

Rhodes Stitches:

These interesting highly textural stitches are great fun and come with many variations. Always start at the same point and go in the same direction for repeat stitches. Rhodes Stitches are hungry stitches and use a great deal of thread (look at the back of your stitch and you will see the build up of stitches as well). To save thread you may come up and down around the outside edge of the edge which will result in a simple outline only on the reverse side but the typical Rhodes Stitch still on the front side.

cushion stitch - bag 5

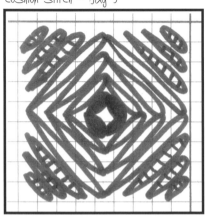

Rhodes stitch   reverse

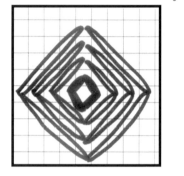

cushion stitch variation #1 - bag 5

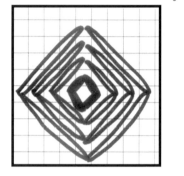

cushion stitch   alternating cushion stitch   counting on the diagonal
                              - bag 9

cushion stitch variation #2 - bag 2   cushion stitch variation #3 - bag 3   cushion block composite - bag 7   diamond eyelet and cushion corners - bag 1

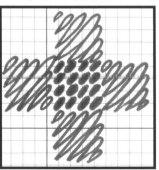

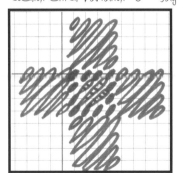

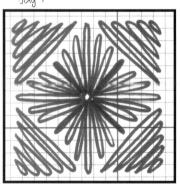

mosaic stitch

mosaic stitch variation #1

mosaic stitch variation #2 - bag 6

Milanese stitch on diagonal

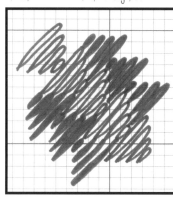

Milanese stitch on diagonal with diagonal satin stitch

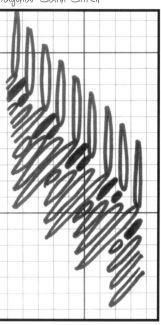

Jacquard stitch - bag 6

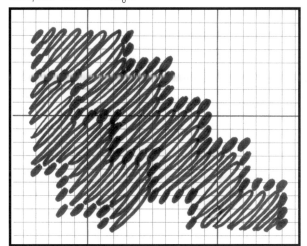

building blocks - bag 6

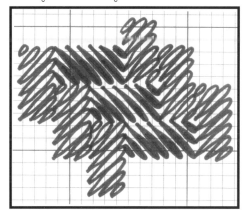

interlocking blocks with unstitched squares - bag 1

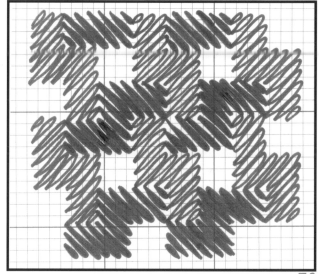

73

notes

FINISHINGS, AND OTHER THINGS

There are many ways of decorating a DÉCOR BAG and those offered in this book serve as an introduction only. You may wish to alter the type of cord or tassels illustrated, add different beads and/or buttons or vary colours. Each DÉCOR BAG is special and the changes you make will add to its charm while making the bag uniquely yours.

- Consider a different type of cord and/or tassel

- Beads are added to all the bags, their sparkle and texture adding another dimension to enhance the visual impact. The colours and types of beads may be changed.

- The composite stitch Raised Stem Band is an ideal stitch for finishing the top edges of the bags – it is easy to do and gives the top edge of a bag a neat finish.

- Other simple embroidery stitches are used too and are illustrated here.

- To enlarge a pattern

Enlarging Templates Summer House Bag #3

On a large sheet of graph paper redraw the grid with each square measuring 2.5cm x 2.5cm (1" x 1"). Add a diagonal line through the grid from one corner to the other. Take each square one at a time and freehand draw the lines as they appear in the smaller grids. Continue drawing these lines until all the shapes are transferred. Those on the graph paper are now ready for colouring with the Transfer Crayons.

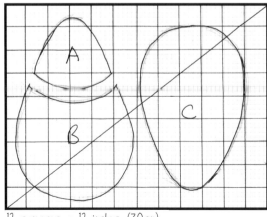

12 squares = 12 inches (30cm)

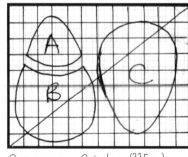

9 squares = 9 inches (22.5cm)

Buttonhole Stitch and Raised Stem Band Stitch

This stitch is used to finish the top edge of all bags except Summer House Décor Bag #3 and the Garden Décor Bag #5. It creates a very clean, neat edge.

In the instructions I generally suggest leaving eight threads at the top edge of each bag. These eight threads are then folded in half to four threads (cut edge is folded to the inside of the bag). *Work Buttonhole Stitch* over and around these four threads, working into every hole of the canvas similar to *Satin Stitch*. Then, using the same colour thread, work *Raised Stem Band* over each pair of *Buttonhole Stitch* 'legs'. Work on both sides of the *Buttonhole Stitch* band, there are usually six rows on each side.

A seamless join in your Buttonhole Stitch may be achieved by leaving the working thread end unsecured. Start a new thread, leave one buttonhole stitch space before continuing the Buttonhole Stitch. When your needle is next free, go back to the thread end and slide in under the first loop of the stitch started with the new thread, then back down in to the canvas along the inside edge. Now secure the thread end.

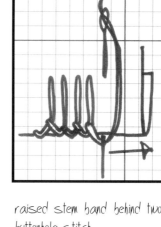

buttonhole stitch

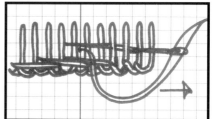

raised stem band behind two 'legs' of buttonhole stitch

bring in a new thread in buttonhole stitch

Additional Backstitch

A simple row of Backstitch between bands of Satin Stitch variations and other similar stitches can be an effective way of adding another colour or accent thread. This is used successfully in the **Music Room Décor Bag #4** where it is placed between the *Raised Stem Band* on the top edge and the Satin Stitch row beneath.

It could well be used in the top band of **Morning Room Décor Bag #1** and down the sides of the central vertical band in the **Drawing Room Décor Bag #6**.

backstitch

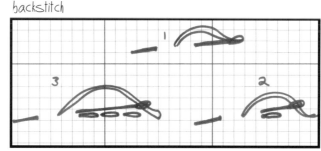

adding one bead

adding a bead using a turning bead

attaching a row of beads

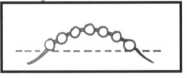

couching down between the beads

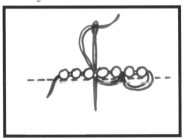

Beads

Beads not only add highlight to the stitching by accenting various patterns but also introduce a change in texture. Most beads are sewn on as individual beads and require a strong thread in a similar colour. Beading needles are not always essential as it is often difficult to thread such small eyes, any sharp needle which passes through the bead will do. Before moving across the back of the work to place the next bead it is advisable to work an extra back stitch on the wrong side to prevent the beads working loose.

When placing a row of beads, such as in the Morning Room Décor Bag #1 it is best to bring the thread out of the canvas, thread the required number of threads onto the needle, then back through the canvas where the row is to end. Then return back along the row couching down the thread in between the beads.

Beads can also look attractive decorating tassels (see p80). They may be stitched individually onto tassels (see Décor Bags #1,3,4,& 6) or threaded onto the fringe while constructing the tassel (see Bag Gallery: Bagman p 78).

Cords

There are many decorative cords available in shops which would be suitable to complete your DÉCOR BAG. The Music Room Décor Bag #4 has a simple black cord; and the Dining Room Décor Bag #6 uses a gold chain clipped from a cheap necklace purchased from a bargain store. However, making your own cord, especially from the threads used within the stitching, will give a better look and compliment your work. They may be used as hanging cords or as part of the finishing as in the Summer House Décor Bag #3 where the cord edges the binding as well.

Basic Twisted Cord

Most of the twisted cords used for the Décor Bags are made up of six or eight thread lengths which will become folded over so that the finished twisted cord will be 12 or 16 threads in total. This means that any cord may be made up of several colours and types of threads – metallic threads look great within a cord, and narrow ribbons may also be used.

Determine the length of the finished cord required and multiply by three. For example a 30cm (12in) finished cord, requires a combination of six or eight threads each 90cm (36 in). I like to add some extra which would make that approximately 100cm (40in). Knot cut ends together, both ends.

Take two pencils and a willing companion, and place pencils between the threads each end while holding the threads taut. Place an even number of threads on each side of the pencils.

Twist the pencils in opposite directions until the twisting threads appear tight (fig 1).
Locate the centre of the twisted cords, hold firmly and slowly bring the two ends together allowing the two sides to twist around each other. Hold cut ends firmly and once the pencils are removed, clamp with a spring clothes peg or knot to prevent unraveling before being stitched in place (fig 2).

The twisted cord ends are securely sewn into the back of the stitched canvas and covered up by the lining fabric.

If you wish to place a tassel at one end of the cord this may be placed onto the threads to be twisted and once the two ends are brought together the tassel will be trapped within the cord (fig 3).

If you do not wish to have a tassel at the end of your cord, simply knot all the threads together and trim ends evenly.

Some clever people use a drill, the bobbin winder on their sewing machines or an electric beater to twist cords and you may wish to experiment with such technology. However, I still favour doing my own, with a 'trained partner'.

Plaited Cord

Plaited cords are ideal too, once again use colours, metallic threads and ribbons selected from your piece. Knot together all the threads at one end and secure to a hook or something firm. Group the threads into three multi-strands and plait firmly (fig 4).

fig 1

fig 2
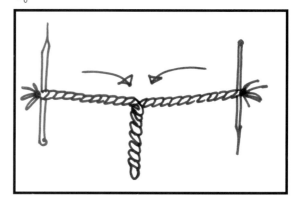

fig 3
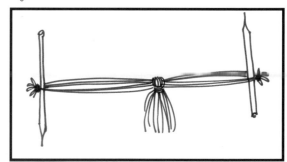

fig 4
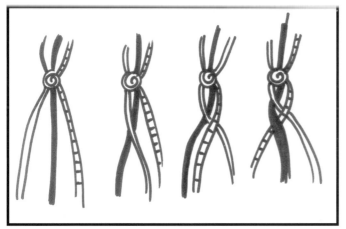

Bag Gallery

These lovely bags were accomplished in DECOR BAG workshops which I tutored.

Annice McPherson

Beverley Christophersen

Elizabeth Foy

Diane Lithgow

Boudoir bag

This bag was worked on one piece of canvas with the four sides extending off a square base. At the time of planning I didn't have sufficient canvas to mark out my template so I turned it into a diagonal cross, with the realisation that any stitches worked on the straight would appear on the diagonal. This presented more problems than initially thought, especially when matching the side seams. Worked in Hand-dyed Hues Variegated thread 506 and other coordinated colours.

Bedroom bag

Worked on an unpainted 18 tpi Camilla Canvas which comes in a soft yellow. Pulled Work (Drawn Fabric) stitches are used successfully and expose the threads of the canvas. Free-standing Detached Buttonhole 'petals' worked over wire; plaited cord.

Bagman

Worked in Hand-dyed Hues Variegated thread 507 and other coordinating colours. Beads and ribbon in amongst the stitch patterns. This bag evolved in design. The face image was not initially planned. The bag does not have a flat bottom but with some manipulation and the help of a ballast of sand (in a plastic bag) it is able to sit upright.

Gallery

Other works on painted canvas

Fifty years after

The ending of World War II celebrated 50 years later. On the left the soldier is symbolised by his uniform jacket, 50 years later he is recognised as a civilian, connected to his past. All in Tent Stitch.

Fish Portrait

Blending of colours and patterns, apart from some Florentine-based lines, all worked in Tent Stitch. Mounted with hand-dyed silk and wrapped thread cardboard.

Hussif cover - *Beryl Callaghan.*

As a result of a workshop I took in using Needlepoint patterns in a Crazy Patchwork format - such fun and wonderful results. Beryl has embellished her piece with tools relating to stitching - ideal for a hussif cover.

Three out of four (marriages) survive.

A criticism of how statistics are always related to the negative (one out of four marriages fail). A strong social comment worked on a painted canvas in Tent Stitch.

fig 1 the simplest tassel

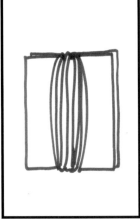

fig 2

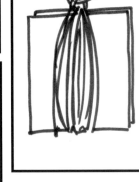

fig 3

Tassels

Tassels give the final 'X' factor to your DÉCOR BAG and may be simple or decorative in style. As for the cords, use threads from within your piece and keep tassels in proportion to the rest of the bag – tassels too large will look heavy, while those too thin will be insignificant.

The Simplest Tassel

Cut two pieces of card the depth of the required tassel. Wrap threads around these cards until the required thickness is reached. Using a needle slip an independent thread length under the threads at one end and knot firmly. Using sharp scissors placed between the cards, cut threads free (fig 1-3). Bind tassel partway down at the 'waist' with another thread and finish off through to the top of the tassel as part of the thread to attach the tassel in place on a bag (fig 4). A single row of Detached Buttonhole may be worked over the binding (fig 5).

Buttonholed Acorn Tassel

This is an old favourite and never fails to please. When binding the 'waist' of a tassel use a long thread and a tapestry needle and once bound securely work a row of Buttonhole stitch over the binding threads. Then work Detached Buttonhole in the spaces of the previous rows, continuing around and upwards decreasing the number of stitches in a row as you work around the top of the acorn (fig 6).

fig 4

fig 5

fig 6

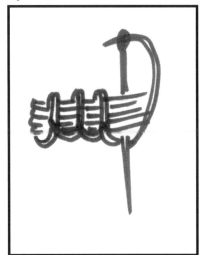

Further ideas:

(a) Add a row of beads to the bottom edges of the Detached Buttonhole stitch (fig 7).

(b) Work a band of Detached Buttonhole Stitch around the 'waist' only and cover with 'ribs' of beads (fig 8).

(c) Do not cut the ends of a tassel but leave as loops and slide wrapped threads off the cards (fig 9).

(d) When wrapping the cards with threads, add a bead on to each thread as you go and do not cut the loops. The beads will hang on loops at the bottom of your tassel (fig 10). See Bag Gallery: Bagman p78.

(e) The tassels on the Morning Room Décor Bag #1 have the hanging cord passed through the tassel and the ends secured with binding. The end loops are covered with Buttonhole Stitch and decorated with beads (fig 11).

(f) The threads at the top end of a tassel may be divided and the threads buttonholed, then bound at the base. This forms a loop through which to pass a cord (fig 12).

fig 11

fig 12

fig 7

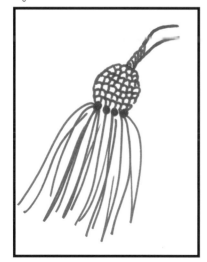

fig 8

fig 9

fig 10

The Joys of Colour

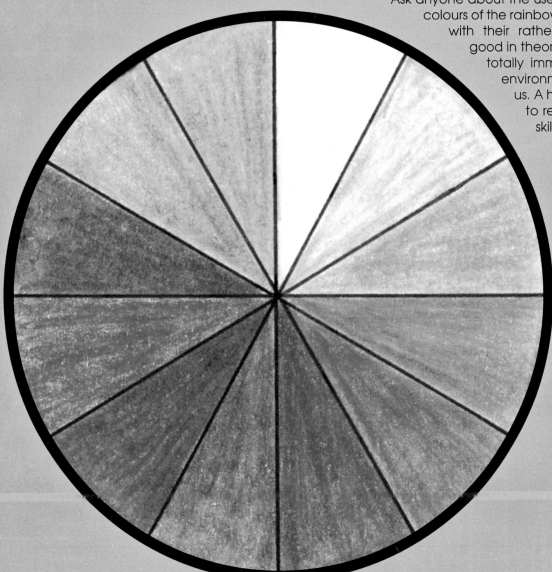

Ask anyone about the use of colour and their answers will be as varied as the colours of the rainbow. Many books and articles are written about colour, with their rather unsympathetic technical approach appearing good in theory, but proving difficult to work with in reality. We are totally immersed in colour everyday in our own man-made environments as well as in the natural habitat that surrounds us. A heightened awareness of observation and the ability to recognise and translate what is seen, is a worthwhile skill to develop.

There seem to be four main aspects of colour that are valuable to embroiderers. Take some time, a random selection of your embroidery threads and test your awareness of the following aspects of colour. In the illustrations opposite I have used colours from a box of 36 coloured pencils, the DEKA Silk Paints applied to paper and threads from my own thread collection.

In needlepoint, as in any embroidery, we also have the added components of texture, the reflection of light on mercerised threads, shiny metallic threads and beads etc, which blended successfully, will compliment the colour component of your projects.

Warm and Cool Colours

Some colours appear to exude more warmth than others, while others appear cold (just think of (red) hot and (blue) cold tap coding before fashion took over and H and C became the alternative). We are all conscious of how we look when we dress in various colour schemes and often this is based on the warmth and coolness of colours. It is simplistic to classify one side of a 12 sectioned colour wheel as warm and the other cold - a red (warm side) may be either warm or cool; a green (cool side) may be also warm or cool. There are even warm whites and cool whites - learn to spot the difference (one will be creamier, the other appears dirty).

Shades and Tints

This is simple, colours that have grey or black added are referred to as Shades, while those with a white component added are called Tints. Any colour may be mixed with white or black and is usually easy to recognise with practice. Try adding some white or black paint to another colour and spot the difference, however when using black only add the smallest amount as it effects are dramatic and irreversible.

Intensity or Saturation

This refers to the depth of colour, its vibrancy and strength. It is not altered by white or black but rather subdued with water to make paler, or pigment added to make stronger.

Highlights or Contrasts

The addition of a limited amount of a contrast colour, carefully selected, will add a spark and life to a colour scheme. This is best in the same shade or tint, and saturation level as the main colour scheme but will come from the other side of the colour wheel ie a warm colour on a cool background, or a cool colour on a warm background.

Warm and cool colours
Deka silk   Pencil

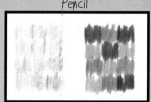

Shades and tints
Deka silk   Pencil

Intensity or saturation
Deka silk   Pencil

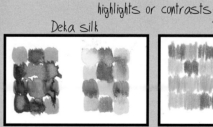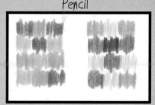

highlights or contrasts
Deka silk   Pencil

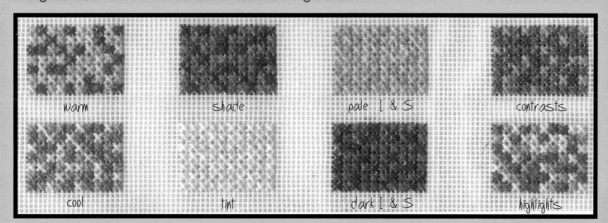

warm   shade   pale I & S   contrasts

cool   tint   dark I & S   highlights

notes

How to design your own DÉCOR BAG

The DECOR BAG designs in this book may be worked as instructed or used as inspiration for designing your own unique DECOR BAG. This is not a difficult task as simply changing the chosen colours to suit your own interior colour schemes will give a quite different look to any of the bags. The Mediterranean Décor Bag, featuring the clear and bright azure colours, may easily be translated to a fresh tangy lemon/lime combination with cerulean blue and magenta to suit a bright room receiving lots of light. The soft colours in Morning Room Décor Bag would be quite restful and peaceful in a combination of blues and greens, with reds to give depth and strength. Try sorting some colours from a particular area of the colour wheel (p82). Take one colour and add the two colours on either side (this becomes an analogous colour scheme), then move across to the other side of the colour wheel and choose the opposite colour (the complementary colour) and as the name implies, a touch of this colour in amongst the others will highlight and lift the appearance of your DÉCOR BAG.

You may wish to keep mainly to one colour. For example the Aztec Décor Bag was stitched with varying shades of yellow and gold highlighted by a touch of lavender, the complementary colour. Colours vary from dark to light and by using a mixture of these different shades and a variety of types of threads (metallic, shiny, twisted, flat) the contrast is sufficient to be satisfying.

Other colour combinations could be quite different and the results quite dramatic. Consider terracotta, pink, lime green, ochre yellow and red/brown, with the terracotta and pink as the main colours and the others used as contrasts. A series of greens with violet, blue/green, blue and warm red would give a totally different look to the same DÉCOR BAG.

Vary the stitch patterns of an existing bag by using those featured in other DÉCOR BAGS and/or the stitch charts. When replacing stitches it is easier if you use others with the same stitch count.

- A row of *Satin Stitch* over four threads could become either a row of *Slanting Satin Stitch* or a row of *Cushion Stitches.*
- A stepped diagonal row of *Alternating Satin Stitch Blocks* could become *Jacquard Stitch.*

Make sure the type of stitch patterns contrast, so that they show rather than blend together, for example a pattern with vertical lines such as *Crossed Satin Stitch* contrasts well with a stitch pattern with an overall grid eg *Blackberry Stitch; Jacquard Stitch* contrasts well with *Double Cross* or *Rice Stitch.*

A diagonal line may be worked in any stitch pattern with diagonal edges eg *Diamond Eyelets* or *Blackberry Stitch.* Fill in any resulting gaps with what would have been there if the complete pattern had been stitched - for example see *Milanese Stitch on the Diagonal* and a row of *Satin Stitch* worked together.

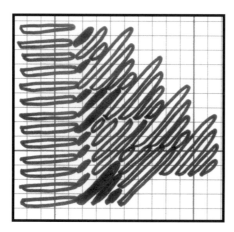

Milanese Stitch on the Diagonal worked beside a vertical row of Satin Stitch - note compensating stitches

Start filling patterns in the centre of any spaces to be filled and work towards the outside edges so that they will all finish with the same part-stitch. When stitching it is always best to complete one area before starting on the next so that unnecessary gaps are avoided and enough space is allowed to complete a stitch pattern. Working stitch patterns with thread counts in groups of four helps to lock patterns neatly together. A space 16 threads wide will accommodate a four-count pattern better than a space with 15 threads.

Designing your own bag by first drawing simple shapes on paper can be an exciting venture. Keep the overall shape simple as the colours, stitches and finishing deservedly take the spotlight. Divide the stitch pattern areas into a few main shapes, keeping the diagonal lines on the true diagonal and plan any curves carefully. Some suggested design layouts for stitch patterns are given on p87.

The stitches may be divided into 'lines' that separate the main shapes giving structure and 'fillings'.

Think about the size of your proposed DÉCOR BAG and its placement on the canvas. Is it to be worked with a fold at the base or does it require a separate front or back? Mark all the lines onto your already coloured canvas using a similar coloured felt pen so that it can just be seen and use the central tacking line for placement.

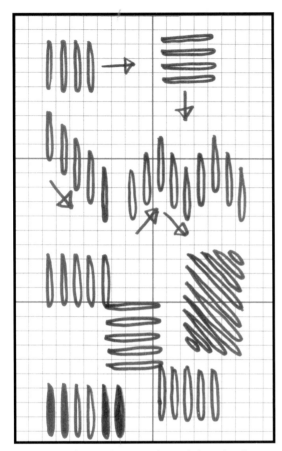

Satin Stitch variations e.g. horizontal, vertical, diagonal, zigzag, alternating

Helpful information to consider when making decisions:

Structure lines	*Satin Stitch* variations, e.g. rows may be horizontal, vertical diagonal, zigzag, alternating *Slanting Satin Stitch* in a straight line *Jacquard Stitch* *Square stitches* e.g. *Cushion Stitch, Double Cross Stitch, Rice Stitch, Mosaic Stitch Variation* *Eyelets - square, diamond*
Fillings	Stripes e.g. any multiples of the above Structure Lines Square grid fillings e.g. *Cushion Stitch variations* Diamond grid fillings e.g. *Blackberry Stitch* All-over repeat patterns e.g. *Interlocking Blocks, Milanese Straight*
Other ideas	Grid and filling patterns look great with the colours of the filling varying as it is worked through the grid Combine similar stitch patterns to create new patterns e.g. Woven Cross Stitch p66 or Off-set Mosaic p69. Mix different types of threads and colours in individual stitch patterns which are composed from several components e.g. Mosaic Stitch Variations p73, Interlocking Blocks p73 etc. Refer to your own library of needlework books for still more Needlepoint Stitches. Leave sections of the coloured canvas showing behind the stitch patterns introduce ribbons, beads and buttons as additional decoration

Designing your own DÉCOR BAG is a further step on your stitching journey, the challenges are worth it and the end result is extremely satisfying.

DECOR BAGS - here are some suggested design layouts for stitch patterns

notes

BIBLIOGRAPHY

Lantz, Sherlee & Lane, Maggie, A Pageant of Pattern for Needlepoint Canvas. Andre Deutsch Ltd, London, 1973

Rhodes, Mary, Needlepoint, The art of canvas embroidery. Octobus Books Ltd 1974

Rhodes, Mary, Dictionary of Canvas Work Stitches. B T Batsford Ltd, 1980

Bahouth, Candace, Medieval Needlepoint. Conran Octopus, 1993

Snook, Barbara, Embroidery Stitches. B T Batsford Ltd, 1963

Cornell, Penny, The Liberated Canvas. Triple T Publishing. 1995

INDEX